THE CHESS PAVILION

Luther Tsai has achievements worldwide as an architect, urban planner, author and academic. From creating spaces in the most vibrant cities of modern Asia to creating innovative Humanities, Science, English and Mandarin curriculum worldwide, Luther and his wife, Serene Pang, the education consultant for this series, recreate the remarkable vision of ancient China found in the Magic Mirror series.

Nury Vittachi is an author based in Hong Kong. His writing is 'endearingly wacky', said *The Times* of London and 'heading for cult status' according to the *Herald-Sun* of Australia. Vittachi has had regular broadcasting slots on the BBC and CNN. 'Dr Who' star David Tennant recently recorded an audiobook version of a Vittachi tale.

For instructions to make the ancient Chinese game, Liubo, go to page 130.

Liubo and Go are among the most ancient of games, that inspired chess and other games that are widely played today.

Liubo board game pattern

Magic Mirror

Mysteries...

The Chess Pavilion

LUTHER TSAI & NURY VITTACHI

SCHOLASTIC
New York Toronto London Auckland
Sydney New Delhi Hong Kong

Thanks to SCHOLASTIC for bringing the amazing stories of Ancient Asia back to life for the world's children to enjoy.

To Frank Wong, Maggie Tan, Selina Lee, Tina Narang, Anukta Ghosh, Himanjali Sankar, Samidha Gunjal, and Daphne Lee, Shin Yee Lim and Fung Teck Hee for going on this visionary voyage together.

The books are dedicated to all fellow adventurers, the educators, parents, youth and explorers who journey with us to rediscover the haunting mystery and history of Ancient Asia inside a Magic Mirror!

Published by Scholastic India Pvt. Ltd.
A subsidiary of Scholastic Inc., New York, 10012 (USA).
Publishers since 1920, with international operations in Canada, Australia, New Zealand, the United Kingdom, India, and Hong Kong.

For information regarding permission, write to:
Scholastic India Pvt. Ltd.
A-27, Ground Floor, Bharti Sigma Centre
Infocity-1, Sector 34, Gurgaon 122001 (India)

First edition: December 2014

ISBN-13: 978-93-5103-708-8

This reprint edition March 2025

Printed in India at Shivam Offset Press, New Delhi

What is Real?

'I sit and gaze on this highest peak of all;
Wherever I look there is distance without end.
I am alone and no one knows I am here,
A lonely moon is mirrored in the cold pool.
Down in the pool there is not really a moon;
The only moon is in the sky above.
I sing to you this one piece of song;
But in the song we are not One.'

From AD 670 Tang Dynasty Poet 'Han-Shan'
which literally means Cold Mountain,
also known as 'Kanzan' in Japanese

Imagine ... a Vision ... a Reflection ... Timeless ...
In the Moonlight.

There is a Place ... On a Mountain ...
A Mirror ... A Book ... and a Curse in the Wind.

Where can you find the mysteries of Ancient China?

Look inside a Magic Mirror.

1

Mountain Flower

OWWWW! A powerful force gripped his torso tightly from behind, squeezing the air out of him. Struggling to breathe, the young man grabbed at the thing that had clamped itself around his body, trying to peel its two sides apart.

'What are you doing?' complained a gruff voice behind him.

'I can't breathe,' the young man gasped. 'I'm going to die.'

'I'm tightening your girdle,' said the man behind, pulling again at the laces that clamped it tight. 'You have to have a girdle, you know. And this type is the height of wedding fashion these days.'

Duke Anchee Daakan Lee shook himself free of the tailor. He attacked the garment around his midriff with some violence, and eventually managed to loosen it before tugging it over his head.

Taking a deep breath, the young nobleman held it between his finger and thumb and gazed at it with disgust for a moment, before tossing it to one side.

The youthful Duke turned to the tailor and opened his mouth to shout angrily at him, but then his shoulders sagged and he let his mouth flop shut. This was his wedding day—no time for a fight. He spoke with quiet exasperation: 'Look, I would really, really prefer to just wear my normal clothes. I'm sure Annee won't mind.'

The tailor raised his eyebrows at this remark, and then spoke with a tone of irritation. 'It's not a matter of what you want or what Annee wants. These things are nothing to do with the youngsters!'

Anchee glared at the older man. 'So our wedding is nothing to do with us? Did I just hear you say that?'

The tailor nodded. 'You did.'

'I thought we were the ones getting married—correct me if I am wrong!'

'You ARE the ones getting married. But it's a wedding! Weddings are not about two people having a bit of a party for themselves. What a ridiculous thought! A wedding is an ancient ritual: it's for the two families involved, it's for the community, it's for society, and it's a legal thing. I mean, ultimately, it's for the continuation of the human race. You have to do it right.'

Anchee looked at the girdle, a mess of cotton layers and

straps on the floor against the far wall. 'But I bet there's nothing in the order of service, however ancient and important it is, that mentions THAT monstrosity.'

The elderly tailor sighed. He was clearly used to young males objecting to the important work he did. Then he glanced at the young man's waist and his expression softened. 'Well, you know, I think we can maybe skip the girdle. You're skinny enough. If we give you a thicker belt than usual, you'll have the requisite hourglass figure.'

Anchee looked confused. 'Why would I want an hourglass figure, pray tell?'

The tailor slapped the Duke's shoulder. 'You youngsters are all the same. You think you're perfect. By pulling your waist in, we make your shoulders and arms look bigger, which makes you look more manly. Your bride will swoon. The official portrait will look great. Nobody appreciates what tailors do anymore.' He spoke this last sentence in a mock sulk.

Anchee folded his arms, unwilling to submit to the man's accusatory mood. 'Look, can you just give me the basics? The requisite cloak and britches or whatever? I just want to get this over with.'

The tailor shook his head, his white beard swinging from side to side as he did so. 'Get this over with'? Let me repeat.

This is not for you! This is for society. This is for humanity. We need to do this properly.' He moved over to the sewing table before continuing in a lighter tone. 'But I must say, your bride is a beautiful young lady, and everyone's favourite. I'm not surprised that you want to make her yours as soon as you can. Yet, I dare say you can afford to take it slow. She's not going to run away.'

The Duke shook his head. 'I'm not worried that she'll run away. That's not the issue. The issue is something quite different. There are many people who don't want us to wed, and who have stood in our way for too long. I'll be happy when this day is over.'

The tailor raised his eyebrows. 'Other suitors for her hand?'

'Certainly, there are other suitors for her hand, but that's not what I mean. There are, shall we say, elements in her own family who would rather that I did not marry her. I hardly think you can be unaware of this.'

'Some things are better not spoken of on a wedding day,' the tailor said, and picked up a cloak. 'Here, let me just check that this is the right length.'

But at that moment, Anchee turned to the window. He held up his hand to let the old man know he should stay where he was. 'I heard something,' he said quietly. 'Something at the window.'

There was a voice calling his name, and a flash of reflected light on the top of the window casement. Someone was shining something from below.

***

The next moment was the first time Anchee had really smiled today—at least since the moment he had woken up and realised that this was the day when he was due to marry Lady Annee at long last.

They had met six months ago in the Chess Pavilion, an open summerhouse at the top of the mountain known as Hua Shan which means Flower Peak, a place where young people gathered to enjoy the view, play games in the sunshine, and fall in love. The spot was breathtaking, as his host, a school friend, had promised.

But once he had seen the two young women playing chess, he lost all interest in the glorious landscape of steep hills and mist-swathed mountains that stretched around them.

One of the girls was tall, elegant and beautiful, with delicate refined features and a bewitching smile. The other was attractive in a different way: she was slightly shorter and rounder, but had a liveliness in her features and a laugh in her voice that grabbed his attention and would not let it go.

The two young men played chess with the two young women most of the afternoon—and before sunset, Anchee was solidly attached to the smaller and younger of the girls, Annee.

From there, the friendship had grown fast, all the way to the choosing of a wedding date—but not without encountering obstacles on the way: a large one in particular. The older sister, Anastasia, was angry that her younger sister was getting married before she was. Such a thing would never have been allowed in the old days, she complained, and family members agreed. Suitors would have been required to propose to the older sister first, and, only if rejected by her, would be allowed to offer their hand to the younger one. That was the way it had been done since time immemorial, Anastasia said.

As a result, there had been much hostility to the young Duke's engagement to Annee. Yet, somehow, the loving couple had persevered with their intention, and seemed to have gradually won over a grudging level of acceptance from other family members, including Anastasia. It had been a difficult journey over the past year, but at last they had reached their destination: this place, this time, this occasion—the day of their wedding.

After having spotted the light flashing at the window,

Duke Anchee Daakan Lee had crossed to the sill and looked down—and gazed into the eyes of his beloved, who was being dressed for the wedding in the same mountainside tower, two floors below.

She had been holding her ritual mirror, an ornamented disk of polished bronze, outside her window, and reflecting sunlight into his room to catch his attention.

The conversation had started with teasing.

'Isn't it bad luck for us to see each other before the wedding?' he had called down.

She laughed before shouting a response. 'It's bad luck for you to see me in my dress. But you can only see my head and a bit of my neck, so that doesn't count.'

'Wait a moment.' He had then gone back into the room and fetched a speaking tube—a sort of long hose—which he dropped out of the window and into her hands. That way, they could have a conversation at normal pitch and not be overheard.

'I still can't believe this is happening,' he said. 'Finally.'

'Yes,' Annee replied. 'It's happening: it really is.'

But it seemed to him that there was something flat in her tone, a lack of enthusiasm. 'What's wrong?' he asked.

'Nothing!'

'You sure?'

'Yes, I'm sure. This is my wedding day. This is the happiest day of my life.'

'Yes. And mine.'

He paused. He felt she was still working just a little too hard to be cheerful. 'But there is something ... something worrying you.'

'No,' she objected with a laugh. 'Silly man, of course not.' A pause. Then she continued in a different tone: 'Well, maybe. It's impossible to hide things from you. But that's how it's meant to be between man and wife, isn't it?'

'Tell me.'

'It's just that ... well ... I'm still finding it hard to believe that Anastasia has agreed to let us do this. It seemed so impossible for so long.'

'It WAS impossible for so long. Think how hard it has been to convince her. Yet we managed it. And Anastasia herself ended up working really hard to organise the event.'

'But still ...' she paused. 'I don't know.' Then she seemed to remember where she was and what she was doing, and her voice brightened. 'Tell me I am being needlessly suspicious. You're my man. That's your job.'

'Then I will do my job. You are being needlessly suspicious,' he declared, not sure if he fully believed his own words.

'You know what? You're right. You're always right. This

is the happiest day of my life and I am letting foolish worries spoil it for me. I'm an idiot. How can you love me?'

'Because you're MY idiot. I'm sending you a gift. Catch this.'

He plucked a small purple flower out of the vase next to the window and dropped it towards her. With a yelp of excitement, she reached out and grabbed it.

'Pin this over your heart,' he said. 'It symbolises your belief in what I just said.'

'Consider it done, noble sir,' she replied. 'Since it comes from you, it will be the most important part of my outfit.' And then she was gone.

***

Duke Anchee Daakan Lee Daaken Lee III spent almost another hour in the chamber before he was finally called to the wedding building.

A small procession of six men—all from her side of the family, since he was from a foreign land—escorted him to the building where the wedding ceremony would take place.

Since the girls' parents were no longer alive, Lady Anastasia and other family members had made most of the arrangements, and had graciously arranged for the Museum of Mirrors to be used as the venue. This was a somewhat odd choice, but ultimately a creative one. The building was grand and stately, and with its circular windows and doors, was attractively distinctive. Besides, circular doorways had always meant 'completeness' in that society, so the building was perfect for the permanent coming together of a man and a woman.

Anchee had reluctantly visited the Museum of Mirrors as a tourist once, soon after his arrival, and had been amazed at what he had seen. He had expected a rather dull collection of historical dressing tables. But what the museum really housed was a collection of rare looking-glasses and metal mirrors, plus demonstrations of the remarkable things you could do with them, from distorting images to creating spaces which appeared 100 times as wide as they really were.

Most amazing was the circular central hall, which housed a display of magic mirrors—ancient Chinese artifacts which were said to have curious properties which baffled scientists. When flooded with light, they gave off curious reflections of lines and shapes which included elements which did not appear to come from any known source. Some said such mirrors had strange powers, or could even work as portals to other places, dimensions or time periods. But clearly that was fantasy, right?

Anchee was curious by nature and insisted on knowing what was behind one room of the mirror chamber which was kept sealed, locked and guarded. He was told that this was the experimentation laboratory. In that room, the chief mirror scientist, Dr Justinian Kutter, had been working with the most powerful of the magic mirrors. There was one, it was said, that really did work as a time portal. It had been hung far overhead so that sunshine from a skylight flowed through it onto a circle painted on the ground. A chicken placed within the beam of oddly shimmering sunlight had disappeared and had been sent back a day later, a dead pile of feathers.

It was said that there had even been two experiments with humans—both condemned criminals who had agreed to the test. One had returned two days later, physically whole but mentally absent. The other had not returned at all. Presumably there was some place in the future or the past which now contained this criminal, either dead or demented.

It was an extraordinary building full of extraordinary things, but had never before been used as a venue for a wedding.

Which brings us back to the present day.

As the Duke and his escorts walked down the mountainside, he heard a rumbling sound in the distance. Thunder? Or some sort of distant landslide? He turned his head to face the sound, which seemed to come from his right, from the west. He saw what seemed to be a flash of light. Lightning? But the clouds were white in that direction. There was no sign of rain. It all seemed a little ominous.

He wanted to pause but the others hurried him on. Probably a good thing. Focus on the job ahead.

Perched on the side of the mountain, the museum was a cluster of concentric circles and semicircles, set off by rectangular towers. They entered through a narrow door on the east side, and the Duke knew that his bride would be entering through a door on the west side at the same time. The timing of their arrivals had been arranged with great care.

Ceremonial music was played as Anchee was escorted through a series of corridors until he stepped into a circular doorway lined with gold, to represent the sun. He faced a large room, the central hall, in which sat the scribes: the officials who would make the wedding legal. Sitting in two rows were Lady Annee's family members who were acting as official witnesses.

He turned his face to his left and waited in anticipation for his bride to appear. To that side was another circular door, partly facing him, but this one draped with flowers. The bride began the ceremony largely obscured, to symbolise the fact that she was separate from him before they were joined.

The music swelled and he saw movement behind the

flowers—and suddenly, there she was, a radiant presence behind the veil of hanging translucent flower petals. She smiled at him and his heart melted. He was suddenly so happy he wanted to cry. To him, her face was unspeakably beautiful. Her dress was stunning, a vision of white with a sheen of mother-of-pearl in elegant vertical lines. But most importantly, today she would become his and his alone forever.

An old man, who looked like a smaller, fatter, less smiling version of the tailor—the long white beard seemed to be a standard element of elderly male society in this part of the world—stepped forward to officiate. He faced them, smiling at the young couple, his back to the witnesses.

'Today you are surrounded by noble persons, all of whom have gathered here to witness your marriage and to share in the joy of this special occasion,' he said in an officious croak. 'Today, as you join yourselves in marriage, there is a vast but unknown future stretching out before you. May it be filled with joy for yourselves, and benefit for your society.'

The old man then turned to address the people in the room. 'You, the witnesses, are here today to play a role in joining these two young people in a life of mutual commitment. It is fitting and appropriate that worthy members of the community should be here to witness this union.'

He turned back to the couple and started talking about rights and duties.

As the speech wore on, Anchee gradually became anxious. He had never been a patient man, and the thought of any official function with lengthy lectures always dismayed him.

He prayed fervently that the service would end soon and he and Annee could get away from this place—and especially from her wild-tempered and unpredictable sister. Talking of whom, where was she? He couldn't see her among the family members seated in the chamber. Perhaps she had decided that she couldn't bring herself to be part of all the celebrations after all. This gave him a pang of guilt. He understood her point of view too. There was logic in having young people married in the order of their birth. But love was love—you can't make it follow the rules

The priest started to intone a long list of official pronouncements, and Anchee tuned out the old man's voice completely, looking into his bride's beautiful eyes. She smiled at him, and his heart melted again.

At last, the droning came to an end, and the service reached its climactic moment. 'The bride and the groom may now join hands and the ring may be transferred. Duke

Anchee Daakan Lee Daakan Lee III, do you agree to love and cherish your bride until death do you part?'

'I do,' he said, and the truth-ring on his third finger glowed greenish-blue.

He watched, his heart filled with happiness, as Annee, only dimly seen through the gently swaying flower curtain, reached her slim right hand through the lines of hanging petals and placed it in his left hand.

Following the tradition of the land, he placed the truth-ring on her finger.

'Lady Annee, Sun of Flower Peak, do you agree to love and cherish your bridegroom until death do you part?'

'I do,' she breathed.

He looked at Annee's pretty face, her laughing eyes, her warm lips, her pale white dress. And there, pinned on the right side of her upper garment was the tiny purple flower that he had dropped from the window.

Something was incited in his mind—something that discomfited him.

What was it? There was a feeling of something being wrong.

His eyebrows knotted. He looked back at her face—it was flawless perfection. Her hair was long, dark, silky. Her lips were full and painted gray-pink, as was the present fashion in this city. Her smile was dazzling. The dress was stunning. The shoes were pointed and sparkled with silvery sequins.

And then he realised what it was. The flower. *The flower.* She said she would pin it over her heart. But it was pinned on the right side of her body, not the left. What could it mean? And the truth-ring: had it glowed blue-green when she spoke? Had it glowed at all?

For a moment he froze.

And then he knew.

2

Mirror Chamber

The young Duke's eyes widened.

He reached for his sword and pulled it out—but what came into his hand was the handle only. Where was the rest of it? It was obviously some sort of dress-sword, with no blade.

He looked back at his bride and at the flower.

'It's a trick,' he said out loud. 'A mirror. Annee, where are you?'

He stretched his arm up high and slammed the bottom of the sword handle against the curtain of flowers that formed the veil in front of his bride—and it hit a hard surface, directly behind the strings of petals, where there should have been empty air.

He slammed it harder—and heard the shattering of glass. The image of Lady Annee, Sun of Flower Peak, looked shocked—and then broke into a thousand pieces of glass.

Yet, in his left hand, her right hand remained.

How could this be?

Unseen hands pulled what was left of the shattered, hidden mirror away to one side.

The curtain of flowers parted—and into the gap stepped Lady Anastasia. It was her hand he had been holding.

The Duke froze in shock.

His mind raced. It was clear that the darkened, candle-lit chamber had been redesigned in a way that had fooled him. Anchee and Annee had somehow been in different rooms—a complex system of mirrors had led them to think they were standing alongside each other. And the hand that had reached for his through the curtain of flowers had not been his bride's hand, but the hand of her sister. He dropped the hand.

'Anastasia!' Duke Anchee Daakan Lee Daakan Lee III exclaimed, with anger evident in his voice.

'That's no way to greet your new bride,' Lady Anastasia said with a cold smile.

'Where is she?'

'Who? My sister? Not here. In a different room. The only man and woman at this altar are you and I, dear boy. And it seems that you have placed a ring on my finger. How nice!'

He turned to stare at the scribes and witnesses—and realised by their furtive, cold, guilty looks that they were all participants in Lady Anastasia's scheme. There was no help to be had by appealing to them.

'But ... '

Lady Anastasia smiled. 'If you are wondering how this was achieved, it was easy. Mirrors, dear boy. I love mirrors. My sister and I have both loved mirrors all our lives. So I got some expert help—from the Master of Mirrors.'

The figure who had taken the pieces of broken mirror away stepped into view. He was a tall man, wide and solidly built: he was the Museum's master, Doctor Justinian Kutter.

Anchee felt strong arms grab his from behind. There had been two soldiers in the shadows, and they had stepped out to hold him in place.

The young Duke turned back to Anna and spoke with fury. 'Why would you do such a thing? Why would you want to be married to someone who doesn't like you? If you are hoping I will eventually fall in love with you, and we'll be happy together, you're crazy.'

Lady Anastasia admired the ring on her finger. 'Oh, I don't think you will eventually fall in love with me. Perhaps I didn't do this to make myself happy. Perhaps I did this to make you and my sister miserable.'

'You are marrying someone who hates you just to create lives of misery?'

'Maybe not lives of misery. Just a week or so of misery. For you, anyway.'

'A week?'

'Yes. The book of the law says that a man who does not fulfill his marriage within a week shall be put to death. The countdown begins. Or of course you could just kiss me. Your choice.'

'You're crazy.'

'My mental state is not the issue here. What we have done is the issue. And what we have done is we have married each other. I'm not doing this for myself. I am doing this for the good of our society.'

He stared at her, his eyes filled with white-hot anger. Then, a thought came to him. 'Wait. A marriage through a mirror is not lawful. It says so in The Record of Ancient Mirrors. And that book has the power of law.'

Lady Anastasia did not visibly react, but her eyes became one shade frostier. She turned to look at Kutter and spoke quietly. 'Kutter?'

'What he says is technically true, Madam,' the Master of Mirrors said, nervously.

She thought for a moment. 'How many copies are there of this book?'

'Just one, my lady. We have the only copy.'

'Bring it to me.'

Kutter hesitated.

'Bring it to me,' she barked.

He bowed his head once, and then slowly went to a side room and returned with an old wooden box. He placed it on a table and opened it. The tall man took out a large, leather-bound volume.

'Give it to me.'

Kutter moved slowly, clearly reluctant to comply. Evidently he felt that this was an extremely valuable piece of Museum property, and he did not want it damaged.

'I said ...' Lady Anastasia began.

'Yes, ma'am,' he interrupted. 'But let us not forget, this is a valuable artifact, my lady, priceless and irreplaceable.'

She took it from him and handed it to one of the guards, a bully of a man named Garth Harshender.

'Put it into that room over there,' she said, gesturing at the experimentation chamber. 'Into the light well at the centre of the room. Under the beam of that mirror thing.'

Kutter looked horrified. 'My lady, if you put it through the portal, the priceless book will be lost forever. We have no control over it. We don't know where it will go.'

'Exactly.'

The Museum director wanted to react but was too scared

to move. By now, Lady Anastasia had a dozen heavily armed guards in the room.

All eyes turned to the bulky soldier Harshender as he approached the locked chamber. Another soldier slashed at the chain with an ax, and the door fell open. Brightness streamed out. A circular mirror was suspended in the ceiling of the room, and a stream of sunshine appeared to be pouring through it.

There were curious lines projected onto the floor—shifting shapes and patterns, and holes which would appear and disappear, as if the ground itself was no longer there. It was a fizzing, shape-shifting vortex of light.

'Throw it in,' Lady Anastasia ordered.

'My lady ...' began Kutter. 'I beg you.'

But it was too late.

Harshender threw the book into the room. There was no thud as it hit the floor—it simply fell into nothingness as if it had been thrown into a bottomless well. The light swallowed it.

Lady Anastasia turned to the young Duke. 'The book you just mentioned ... it was lost ... recently.'

Duke Anchee Daakan Lee thought for a while before replying, 'If it is lost, then it can be found.'

Lady Anastasia responded, 'It cannot be found, because

it isn't anywhere. Not in this world. You don't really understand magic mirrors, I see. The book is not lost in space. It is lost in *time*. It may have reappeared a long time ago in history. Or it may have gone into the future, in which case it hasn't existed yet.'

'You're insane.'

She gave him a look filled with a mixture of emotions, including love, lust and cruelty. 'People with hearts full of love are usually described as mad. I don't mind. I may be insane, but it is better than being dead. You can choose to do things my way—or you can choose to be jailed for a week of misery and then put to death.'

'Your scheme is crazy. How can you even imagine that you can achieve anything with this sort of plan?'

'I have already achieved a lot. Your face is a perfect picture of misery, just as I knew it would be.'

'Oh, this is not misery. This is determination. Determination to prove you wrong.'

'It looks like misery to me. And fear. And despair.'

Duke Anchee Daakan Lee smiled. 'Show me, then,' he said to the mirror master. 'You have plenty of mirrors, right?'

Kutter turned to Lady Anastasia for permission. She nodded and he brought one of the circular metal mirrors over to where the guards were holding him.

It was Lady Anastasia's first mistake.

Duke Anchee Daakan Lee Daakan Lee III used his steel-shod heel to kick the knee of the guard who was holding him, then shook himself free and grabbed the metal mirror.

Using it as a weapon, he swung it at Kutter, and it hit him with a loud *clang*! The blow knocked him off his feet. Anchee turned and batted the nearest guard with it. He raced away across the chamber, towards the room, the experimentation chamber where the book had disappeared.

'It's too late. The book has gone,' shouted Lady Anastasia. 'Step through the portal and you'll disappear too.'

The Duke spun on his heel to defend himself as other guards reached him. He fought bravely, using the mirror as a shield, but the odds were clearly impossible. There were at least a dozen guards approaching him in a semicircle.

They moved slowly towards him, a wall of metal-clad muscle. Behind him, in the laboratory, was the vortex and probable death. In front were Harshender and the rest of Lady Anastasia's guards—certain death.

'You can't escape,' said Lady Anastasia, speaking in a conciliatory tone. 'Your time is up, Duke. You have nowhere to go.'

'Then I will find another time and another place,' he said.

Still clutching the circular metal mirror in his hands, he

turned and threw himself into the vortex.

As he fell towards the hole, he saw Lady Anastasia's cold face. She opened her mouth to scream.

But behind her, he saw movement. It was his beloved bride. Sweet Lady Annee, struggling between two guards, had been brought into the room. She was watching him fall into the vortex. The last thing he heard before he blacked out was the wail of horror that burst from her lips.

3

Books and Other Curiosities

A very great distance away to the south, or perhaps the north, and a very long time afterwards, or perhaps much, much earlier, a scene more recognisable to you and I, dear reader, was taking place: two young people were heading home from after-school activities as the sun was setting.

Miranda Lee wearily climbed the porch steps of the old house and fumbled with her key to open the front door. As the lock clicked, her younger brother Marko pushed the heavy wooden door, and it swung open with a creak like one of those scary TV horror shows.

The girl reached for the light switch as her brother scampered into the house. 'I need the toilet,' he squealed as he galloped away into the gloom.

'I'll alert the media,' she said, using a joke that she had heard in some old movie.

Her hand touched a piece of paper. A note had been taped on the light switch—obviously placed there so that they would find it as soon as they came home.

She turned on the light and read the note. The message on the small square of paper was in the handwriting of Mrs Gwendy, the housekeeper who visited every other day.

'Miranda and Marko, your grandfather sent you a pair of books. I put them on the table in the living room. Be sure to write a thank you note.'

Miranda smiled. *Yeah, right. As if we'd know where to send a thank you note.*

She started to put down her school bag, but then had a thought. The note said, a 'pair of books'. She had better go and check them out in case one was better than the other. For it would only be right for her to have the better one, given the fact that she was the older child. It was her privilege and right to have the first choice for everything because she had got here first, right?

In the freshly dusted living room, she found two very different books on the table. One was about games and the other seemed to be a poetry collection.

She snatched up the games book. 'Well, this one can be for me,' she said out loud to no one in particular. Ha! It had been a good move to get in quick and choose first. Most people would have been horribly sexist and assumed that a book about a fun subject like games would be for a boy, and a boring volume of poetry for a girl.

She saw the large envelope nearby in which the books had arrived. There was no return address and no letter inside. But her grandfather's handwriting on the label was unmistakable.

Thirteen-year-old Miranda Lee sat on the sofa with her book safely in her hands and then called out to her brother. She heard him flush the toilet.

'Marko. Grandpa sent us presents. In the living room.'

The boy appeared, wiping his hands on his school shorts.

'What are they?'

'He sent us some books.'

'Cool.'

'Yours is a poetry book.'

Marko picked it up and arranged his thin limbs on one of the dining chairs, flicking through the pages. 'Is yours the same?' he asked.

'No,' she replied. 'He sent me a book about games.'

She waited for him to express irritation, or at least suspicion, but he didn't. Her brother was infuriating that way, probably deliberately.

As she glanced over, she saw that he was simply turning the pages of the poetry collection and reading random pages.

She looked down at her own book. It was called *Games,*

Ancient and Modern. She turned to the opening chapter and read the first paragraph.

It started by defining what a game was, describing it as 'a competitive activity played according to a list of rules or limitations and usually decided by a combination of skill and luck'.

Miranda started to worry. Perhaps this wasn't going to be a fun book, after all. It seemed to be a *study* of games. Rather serious. Why couldn't grandpa have just sent her a game, instead of a book about games?

She looked over at her brother, but he seemed engrossed in his book. 'How's your book? Is it interesting?' she asked, hoping for a negative answer.

He nodded. 'Did you know that there was a poet called Jack Kerouac who wrote a book that was all on one giant sheet of paper, like a toilet roll, 36 meters long? That's like 10 cars long.'

'It seems you can't talk about anything except toilet-related things at the moment.'

He ignored this comment. 'The guy stuck a huge number of sheets of paper together and wrote this long thing with no paragraph breaks or chapter headings or anything. Just one long paragraph that was longer than a bus.'

He flicked through a few more pages and read another

paragraph. 'And there was a guy called H.P. Lovecraft who wrote scary stories and poems, and became famous. Some were made into horror movies. And there's a whole chapter on funny poems. And did you know that some of the first poems ever written were from India and China?'

Miranda's eyebrows wrinkled crossly. 'I think that book is meant to be for me, and this one is meant to be for you.'

He looked over at her.

She held up the book of games. 'This is about the history of games. Definitely a boy thing. That poetry book is meant for me. Poetry is a girl thing. Everybody knows that.'

Marko flicked to the front of the book in his hands. 'There's no name on the inside cover. I guess we could share both books.' He went back to reading the text.

Miranda sighed and looked down at the book in her hand. She would have one more try at getting into it, she decided. And then if that didn't work, she would go and do something else. She started reading.

Games had always been really important to humanity, the book said, and some of the oldest artifacts known to man were games.

In ancient Egypt, they played a board game called Senet, and copies had been found which were more than 5,000 years old—which is pretty much as old as recorded history. In a place called Burnt City in Iran, an ancient backgammon set had been found, which was of similar age.

Miranda pictured pharaohs and those other ancient dudes all sitting around playing Monopoly or whatever the equivalent was in those days. It's human nature to want to relax and have some fun after a hard day's work, right?

Mira flicked through the pages to look at the pictures and was surprised when a note fell out—a letter in grandpa's handwriting.

'I got a note from grandpa!' she said, lifting it to eye level.

There were just four words on it: 'Miranda, read chapter three.'

She flicked to chapter three and found it was a description of some of the oldest games in the world. It started off by talking about something called Liu Bo, an ancient game from China which was sometimes found carved onto the back of .... magic mirrors!

Okay, now this was beginning to make sense. Grandfather had sent them on several explorations involving magic mirrors and history—so it looked like this could be another one.

Miranda sprang to her feet and strolled over to Grandpa's study, to see if their Magic Mirror looked anything like the one in the diagram in her book.

***

Marko turned his book upside down and was browsing through the pages to see if he too had a note. There wasn't one. But then he found a note written on one of the blank pages at the start of the book.

His note was very different from his sister's—and baffling. It said: 'Urgent! Go to the great mountain of poems tonight and tell Cold Mountain that the answer to the question is "Lady Annee and The Record of Ancient Mirrors".'

Now, *that* was interesting. Clearly, Grandpa had a job for them—and an urgent one too. He ran into the study to find his sister standing by the window holding the Magic Mirror of the Moon, an ancient artifact that had been sent to them by grandfather, six months ago. She looked at the words that appeared around the rim after every full moon adventure. They now read: 'Look Time Coming Devil Woman.'

'We've got a mission,' Marko said. 'We've got to go to a place called Cold Mountain and deliver a message—tonight.'

They looked at the ancient mirror Grandpa had entrusted them with. A magic mirror is a curious object. It's possible you have seen them in museums, or sometimes in the homes of private collectors—but it's at least equally probable that you've never encountered one. Most people have never heard of them.

Magic mirrors are ancient metal-reflecting surfaces from

China. A typical example would be a mirror polished on one side and ornamented on the other. These items can be used for normal mirror purposes—you can look at your face in them. They are generally circular, or sometimes flower-shaped, and some have rippled edges.

But they have other strange properties too, which have baffled scientists for centuries. When you put one in a brightly lit space, or shine a beam of light on one, the light reflected through it or off it appears to contain lines or textures.

Some say the light shines through the mirror, and the lines projected match the pattern on the back of the mirror.

Others say the light reflects off the front of the mirror—and somehow picks up the lines of the back of the mirror, although it is not clear how.

And there are other mysteries too. Sometimes the lines projected by the mirror are not the lines on the back of the mirror at all, but different shapes or images. So where do they come from?

Marko and Mira could only begin to guess after strange adventures with Grandpa's unusual mirror. It was called the Mirror of the Moon, and was not meant to be used in sunlight, but at night.

The two children would hold the mirror up to the moonlight and something bizarre would happen—although not everyone agrees what this was. Their teacher says that this was how the children began an imaginative game in which they pictured themselves in the place they'd been studying or talking about. But the children had a different story. They said that the Magic Mirror really took them to a different time and place. The adults, as always, were doubtful, but who knows for sure?

***

'We need to go now,' Marko said. 'The note says that we have to do it this evening. It says it's urgent.'

'But where are we going? I don't know if I want to go anywhere this evening. I have a book to read.'

'We have to do it tonight.'

She sighed. 'Okay, okay, keep your hair on. Where are we going?'

'We're going somewhere called Cold Mountain.'

'We'll need to put on our jackets, then.'

She went into the hallway and grabbed the two coats hanging on hooks near the door.

Her brother was impatient. 'Come on,' he said. 'We gotta go.'

'Can you wait? I think we should take some snacks or something.'

But before she could move to the kitchen, Marko held up

the mirror and the moonlight from the window was filtered onto his face and the surfaces behind him. Mira instinctively joined her brother, so that both were standing in the circle of light. It became increasingly bright.

She saw lines and colours around her—and they shifted, stretched and spread. From her point of view, there really was something magic about magic mirrors.

The room around them seemed to fade away. The brightness turned to white light, and she could see nothing at all. But she knew that soon they would be in the midst of different surroundings. They were on their way.

4

Silent Graffiti

Reality flowed back. As their eyes were adjusting to the new place, the first thing that hit them was the cold. They instinctively wrapped their arms around themselves. It was like being dropped into a freezer.

'Brrrr! Thank goodness I brought the jackets,' said Mira, proudly. 'Another good idea of mine. I'm full of them.'

Marko, blinking, was paying no attention to his sister, but absently put on the jacket she had handed him. He placed the mirror into his red school backpack and then gazed around.

As their eyes came back into focus, they saw they were on a winding path which cut away steeply on one side. But the downward slope was thickly forested, so it was hard to tell how high they were. They were definitely on some kind of hill or mountain. The temperature suggested they were high up—as did the cutting wind that lifted their hair and made the trees sway.

'This must be the mountain of poems that is mentioned

on Grandpa's note,' the boy said, half talking to himself. He turned to his sister. 'But I wonder why he calls it that. It just looks like a mountain of rocks and stuff, like any normal mountain. Not a mountain of poems.'

'Well, what do you think it would look like?' Mira asked. 'A gigantic pile of words or something? That would be silly.'

'Yes, but why is it called a mountain of poems if it is just a regular mountain?'

'Who cares? We need to just do our job and get back. It's too cold to hang around here very long. I think it was a really bad idea of yours to get us here before we were fully prepared. I was going to go and get some snacks.'

'The note said we had to deliver the message urgently this evening.'

'Look, I wasn't ready. You brought us here too early. And to make up for it, I am going to be the undisputed leader on this trip, okay?'

'You always are, anyway. You're so bossy.'

'Yeah, but this time, I am not going to need to be bossy because you are going to submit automatically to the fact that I am the natural leader of this community.'

'This community?'

'Us.'

'Oh right. So you're the boss of me?'

'Yes.'

Marko thought about replying but then decided not to. He was a practical boy and he had had this type of argument with Miranda too many times to pay it much heed.

He looked at the note in his book and read it out loud: 'Urgent! Go tonight to the great mountain of poems and tell Cold Mountain that the answer to the question is, 'Lady Annee and The Record of Ancient Mirrors'.'

Mira asked, 'So, is this Cold Mountain?'

'I guess so. It's a mountain and it's cold.'

She pulled her jacket around her more tightly. 'It's a bit chilly but I've been in colder places.' The girl looked around, watching the branches sway.

'So go on then,' her brother said, handing her the book.

'Go on what?'

'Tell the mountain the answer to the question.'

'Tell who?'

'Tell the mountain. That's what it says in the note.'

'That's stupid. You can't tell a mountain something.'

'Why not?'

'Because it's a mountain. It's not going to listen, is it? Idiot.'

'But you tell me stuff, and I don't listen. It doesn't stop you.'

Miranda Lee's eyebrows furrowed crossly. 'You say it.'

'I thought you were the leader of us.'

'I'm in charge of stuff that's not silly. The silly stuff I delegate to you. To my subordinate. That means you.'

She handed him the book. 'There's the message. Tell the mountain.'

The boy sighed and took the book back from her. 'Okay, I'll do it. Hello, mountain. Can you hear me? I don't know if you can hear me or not, but I've been told to tell you something. The answer to the question is 'Lady Annee and the Record of Ancient Mirrors'. Does that mean anything to you?'

He waited. There was silence.

Mira, as always, was impatient. 'Come on, let's go. This is silly. We need to deliver the message to a human.'

'Where should we go? Wait. I think I can hear something.'

'What?'

'The wind.'

She listened for a moment. 'It's not saying anything. It's just blowing. Come on, let's go. Mountains can't talk, so they certainly can't discuss questions or tell us stuff.'

It seemed wise to walk, if only to generate warmth. So they marched ahead, following the path and going up and down stone staircases from time to time. After walking for a few minutes, they had warmed themselves up. Then they turned a corner and stopped dead. There, clearly written on the rocks, was a lengthy piece of writing.

'Graffiti—that's naughty,' said Mira. 'Spoiling a country park is illegal.'

Marko scratched his chin thoughtfully. 'Maybe it's not graffiti. Maybe that's the mountain's reply.'

'What do you mean?'

'Maybe it just appeared after I asked the question.'

'That's crazy. It's probably been there for years.'

They approached the writing. It appeared to be a line from a poem.

'Reality is asking the shadow the way.'

Mira pondered for a while, and then said, 'It's definitely not graffiti. Graffiti says things like A.B. loves C.D. It's a bit of a poem. Anyway, graffiti like that is no help to anyone. I wish the local graffiti writers would write something simpler. Like "You Are Nearly There. Turn Left For Snack Shop".'

"Turn left for snack shop" is not poetry.'

'It would be poetry to me,' she replied.

***

They walked for another ten minutes along the winding mountainside path before meeting another traveller—a man in robes. He had a kindly look about him, and smiled and nodded as he walked past.

Mira decided to speak to him. 'Excuse me, sir, can you tell us where we are?'

The man turned and smiled again at them, but said nothing. He then continued on his way.

'Maybe he didn't understand,' Marko said. 'They probably have their own language here. Let's try someone else. Look.'

Further down the path, they saw two more men approaching, also in robes.

'Excuse us, can you tell us what this place is called?' the boy asked.

The men stopped and looked at each other for a second. Then one of them pointed to his closed mouth. The other drew something in the air with his finger—it was unclear whether it was a picture or a word.

Miranda asked her brother, 'Are you guys mute or something? Can't you talk?'

'If they were mute, they couldn't tell you,' Marko said in a whisper. 'Maybe they took a what-do-you-call-it? A promise not to talk kind of thing? They're monks, right? The robes suggest that, right?'

'A vow of silence.' She looked at the man who had pointed to his mouth. 'Have you guys taken a vow of silence?'

He nodded.

She looked faintly annoyed and then said, 'Look, all

respect to your rituals and all that, but would you mind just telling us where we are and then you can, you know, shut up again for the rest of the day?'

'I don't think they can do that,' her brother said.

Mira continued to talk to the men. 'We wouldn't tell anyone. Cross our hearts and hope to die.'

Marko said again, 'I don't think they can do that.'

'I'm just asking! It's okay to just ask!'

The two men looked blank at her request.

Mira threw up her hands. 'Never mind. We'll ask someone else.'

The two men looked at Miranda and shook their heads.

'What do you mean? Do you mean it's no good to ask someone else?' She winced. 'You're not telling me that everyone on this mountain has taken a vow of silence?'

The men nodded.

'But that's so inconvenient. What about the tourist trade? Don't you guys care about visitors? This is an outrage.'

They looked baffled.

Then one of the men pointed in the direction in which they were going and made a beckoning gesture with his other hand.

'They want us to go with them,' Marko said.

'I'm not stupid—I can work that one out,' his sister said.

'Maybe there's someone back at their HQ or whatever who is allowed to talk to tourists. Like a tourism information desk. I can't believe how dumb this is. Someone should complain to someone.'

***

They soon reached a sort of monastery-temple complex and one of the monks took the two children around to the back entrance. He pointed towards something in the distance. There were two much smaller stand-alone buildings on the crest of a small dip in the valley-side.

Mira put her hands on her hips and told her brother, 'Well, there seem to be only three buildings on this mountainside, so it shouldn't be too difficult to find the right place to deliver our message. We just need to visit each of the buildings in turn and tell people about our mission until it clicks with someone.'

Marko looked unsure about the plan. 'But how can we learn anything if people here aren't allowed to talk or reply?'

She cupped her chin with her finger and thumb. 'Good point. Sign language?'

The men continued to point to the two smaller houses, rather than the main temple.

'Maybe they are pointing to those buildings because that's where people are allowed to talk,' Marko said. 'Let's go see.'

A few minutes later, as they reached the first of the two buildings, they saw a woman walking along the path in front of it. But when she caught sight of them, she stopped and waited for them at a small junction of several paths.

'Welcome,' she said. 'Are you attending training today?'

'You can talk?' This was Mira. 'Hooray!'

'Yes. People associated with training are allowed to speak. Otherwise how could the monks train people?'

'So ... people in the training section ... we could tell them things, and they could reply?'

'Yes.'

'That's where we want to be. We need to find the right person and tell them something.' She addressed her next comment to her brother. 'So now we know we're not meant to be in the main building where no one can talk. That's one out of three buildings knocked off our list.'

The woman pointed to the third building. 'Go to that building over there. That's for the young people. I'm sure that's where you're meant to be.'

She addressed this last comment to Marko. Then she turned to look at Mira. 'As for you, you can wait outside, or go and help in the monastery kitchen.'

'What do you mean?'

'Well, you're obviously not allowed in the training rooms.'

'Because?'

'You're female.'

'I'm not allowed in because I'm a girl? That's *so* sexist!'

The woman looked puzzled, unfamiliar with Mira's term. But the girl's angry tone had been unmistakable. She added, 'Women can't train to be monks here. But there is a women's community in the next valley, if you also want to take up the same sort of training. Men are not allowed there.'

'That's fair,' said Marko. 'But you're a woman. How come you're allowed here?'

'I'm not a member of the temple. My official job is that of a 'Mobile Signpost'. I help travellers who pass by.'

'You're the tourism information desk sort of thing,' said Mira.

The woman looked puzzled again.

'Don't worry. That's what we call people who do your job where *we* come from.'

The woman looked directly at Mira and said, 'There's another thing. Some strange people have been seen on this side of the mountain in the past year or so. You children are probably safer going to the women's community.'

'Thanks,' said Marko, before grabbing his sister's arm and tugging her away. 'Thanks for your help. We better go now. We don't want to be late. My sister can wait outside the training building for me.'

They raced towards the furthest structure, but as soon as they were out of sight, they ducked behind some trees.

'Do you want to wait here for me?'

'No way,' said Mira. I'm going in with you.'

'How?'

'I'm going to change my gender. Just wait and watch.'

5

Studious Skeptics

Miranda Lee spent the next few minutes loosening her clothes to make them baggy and shapeless, and then she put up the hood of the red hoodie she was wearing.

'Tuck your hair in,' Marko said.

'It is tucked in.'

'Tuck it all in. You still look like a girl.'

'I am a girl, idiot.'

'But you mustn't look like one.'

Mira's voice took on a haughty tone. 'I know how to play a boy. I was Robin Hood in the school play when I was nine. It's all about how you walk.'

She lumbered heavily in a straight line across the clearing in the trees, swinging her shoulders from side to side, thudding her feet into the ground.

Marko folded his arms. 'That's not how boys walk. You look like, I don't know, a rugby player or The Hulk or something.'

'Rugby players are boys. The male ones, anyway. And The Hulk.'

'That's not how I walk. I'm a boy.'

'You're a child,' she said.

Again Marko decided not to take the bait.

Mira borrowed some sort of brown sheet from a washing line at the side of the building and tied it round her, making a robe. And then they started to walk around towards the front.

There was a sound from the house.

A tiny slit in the door creaked open and a pair of eyes became visible.

'Would you mind opening the door?' said a voice from inside.

'What?' Mira asked.

'Would you mind opening the door? There's no handle on the inside, you see. You have to open it from outside.'

'You're locked in?' She reached for the handle and opened the door. 'Is this like a prison?'

'Come inside, boys,' said a teacher, who appeared to be in his mid-20s. 'We're ready for you.'

He ushered them in.

'Why is there no ...?' Mira began, and then restarted her question, speaking at a lower pitch with a gruffer tone, trying to sound more masculine. 'How come there's no handle on the inside of the door?'

The youthful teacher explained, 'As a sign of humility, we put the handles on the outsides of doors only, to acknowledge that we are in training, and follow the instructions of our seniors.'

'It's kind of strange.'

The teacher smiled. 'It is—you're right. And there is another reason too,' he said. 'Some of the students don't want to study and beg us to release them. If we tell them that we are unable to open the door until someone comes at the end of the day, then they stop pestering us about it and get on with their learning.'

Mira asked, 'What about health and safety?'

The young monk looked puzzled. 'What?'

'I mean, fire safety regulations and so on?'

Marko added, 'Yeah, what if a fire broke out and you needed to leave?'

The monk said, 'In an emergency, we could probably break the doors or windows down in a few minutes—they are not very strong.'

The girl said, 'Still, it seems strange.'

The man turned to them and raised his eyebrows. 'I will tell you a little secret. We may change the policy quite soon.

There have been reports of troublemakers in the area. A pair of vandals has been seen in the district several times. We're thinking we may put the handles back on the inside of the doors until they've left the area. We have to be very careful. There has been a prophecy that two of the monks here will live forever. So we have to look after ourselves. Of course, we don't know which two—so we are all being very careful. Now here's the classroom.'

The two children entered a medium-sized room and sat down on the floor.

The boy asked, 'Are we the only students, sir?'

'There'll be a few more in a moment, so just settle down and get ready.'

There were no desks. They sat on earth that had been pressed flat. It was actually not too uncomfortable. Marko wondered why this was so. Perhaps humans had sat on mud and grass for so long in history that soft, packed-earth floors were actually more comfortable than the hard-tiled or parquet floors that many modern people have.

After four or five other young men arrived and joined them, the teacher began his lessons.

'I am Brother Teh and this is my colleague, Brother Sek. He pointed to a small, stocky man in the corner who was lifting a small dumbbell with one arm.

'I am the junior master and he is known as the healthy skeptic.'

'Very healthy as you can see,' said Brother Sek, flexing his biceps.

'Two teachers for one class?' Mira asked.

'The policy at this house of learning is to have a healthy skeptic to work alongside each teacher so that students get a balanced view, and nothing ever gets twisted too far to one side or another because of a teacher's particular interests or predilections.'

'That sounds like a good idea,' whispered Marko.

'Yes, remember when Ms Chappell took up knitting and talked about nothing else?' Mira asked.

'Or Mr Pandit and the sports results, which had to be discussed everyday?'

'No talking, please!' the monk at the front of the classroom scolded.

The healthy skeptic added, 'You cannot talk while the teacher is talking, although it may be a good idea to have discussions during periods where students are collaborating on something.'

Then Brother Teh made an unexpected request. 'Okay, what would you like to study?'

'Do we get to choose?' Marko asked.

'Yes, we always begin with what is called the test of mastery,' Brother Teh said. 'The students suggest a topic and the master has to make an instant presentation on it. This confirms the teacher's right to be the teacher.'

Mira raised her hand. 'Do you know anything about someone called Lady Annee or a book called *The Record of Ancient Mirrors*?'

Brother Teh thought for a moment. 'No,' he said.

Mira looked around the room. No one else had reacted to her question. 'Okay, games ... can you tell us about games?'

'Games? Hmm. That's an interesting one. I don't think that has ever been suggested before,' Brother Teh said.

'That doesn't count as a philosophical topic,' the healthy skeptic complained.

Brother Teh raised one finger to signify that he disagreed. 'It does in a way. Let me put it this way. It has long been known that games are very good for mental exercise—some say they provide you with the best mental exercise you can possibly get. So people have long played games to sharpen their wits.'

He warmed to his theme. 'Now, the very first games in this part of the world were Liu Bo and Go, two board games which are related to each other but played differently. These have been popular for centuries, and have spread to the rest of the world. Some other games have been built related to them. Some say that chess, the game that is particularly popular in countries in the far west, is derived from Liu Bo.'

He drew a design on a large piece of slate which was obviously their equivalent of a whiteboard. 'Liu Bo, which means six sticks, is generally played on a special board with markings on it,' he said.

'This is kind of boring,' Mira whispered to her brother.

'Sometimes you see these same markings on magic mirrors,' the teacher continued.

She turned back to him, her attention caught. Perhaps their Magic Mirror was actually a board game. That might explain some of the strange symbols and numbers on it.

'Please, sir,' she said, raising her hand again. 'My brother and I have a Magic Mirror. Is this a board game? Show him.'

'Huh?'

'Show him our Magic Mirror.'

Marko fumbled to get it out of his backpack.

Brother Teh stepped over to the where the children sat and took the mirror from their hands. He looked at it with wide eyes. 'This is a beautiful example of a traditional magic mirror, probably centuries old. Where did you get it?'

'It belongs to our grandfather. He gave it to us,' Marko said.

'It's wonderful. Now, students, who can tell me something

about magic mirrors?'

The students looked baffled. One at the very back put up his hand and said, 'They are magic, I'm guessing?'

'Good guess. Magic mirrors are indeed magic.'

'Wait, wait, wait, wait.' This was the healthy skeptic. 'I don't think I like the word 'magic'. It is not very scientific. Can we find a better word?'

Brother Teh thought for a moment. 'Would magical be alright?'

The healthy skeptic thought about this. 'Yes, I guess magical will do.'

The students by this time had started to get interested. 'So what makes a magic mirror magic?' one student asked. 'Or magical?' he added, with a sidelong glance at the healthy skeptic.

'May I?' asked Brother Teh, moving away with Marko's magic mirror.

He held it up to the window.

'Sunlight falls on the mirror. It is reflected back from the shiny side. But some people say the mirror also works as a filter. Sunlight falls on the back and goes straight through. Lines are projected on the opposite wall.'

'Which is impossible, of course,' said Brother Sek, doing his job of being a healthy skeptic. 'The metal is too thick for light rays to get through.'

'Which may *seem* impossible,' added Brother Teh. 'But it does seem to work. Some people say that the mirror is made of special metal that lets light through. It may travel via too-small-to-see gaps between the particles that make up the object, tiny bits of material that the Greeks have dubbed atoms. Others say that the mirrors are so reflective that in a light-filled area, the light seems to go through, but is really just being reflected from the front.'

The healthy skeptic thought for a moment whether this was acceptable, and then decided that it was. He gave a sort of half-scoop gesture with his hand that appeared to mean 'Carry on.'

'What about the lines?' asked Mira. 'Aren't they the most magical thing of all?'

Brother Teh nodded. 'Yes. Your grandfather has taught you well. The lines, of course.' He held up the mirror in the sunshine pouring through the window.

'In bright light, there are patterns and markings on the back which appear on the wall or floor as if they were projected. This may be because the mirror is acting as a light filter, or this may bounce light from the front, although there are no visible markings on the front. This creates an unusual visual effect.'

He looked at the healthy skeptic. The small, muscular man rubbed his chin for a while and then gave the 'carry on' sign again.

'The lines which are projected or reflected on the walls apparently come from the back of the mirror.'

The healthy skeptic raised his hand. 'Isn't there some sort of theory that the patterns on the back make very fine lines on the front? So you can't actually see the lines, but they are there?'

Marko's hand shot up. 'I saw a thing on TV about laser printing of circuits. The lines are so fine, you can't see them, but they are there.'

Mira elbowed him and whispered, 'That's dumb. They don't have laser printing here.'

'I know.'

'What is lazy printing?' Brother Teh asked.

'It's a machine we have where we come from that prints things so fine and so small that you can't see them. But they are there.'

'Interesting. I would love to see one of these machines.'

Mira was not sure how to reply. 'When we come back this way next time, maybe we can bring you one.'

'Let us continue,' said Teh. 'The interesting thing—and perhaps we can call it the magical thing—is that sometimes the lines projected out of the magic mirror do not correspond to the lines on the back of the mirror—they seem to come from nowhere. That's the most magical thing of all.'

'Ours does that,' said Mira proudly.

'It sure does,' Marko added. 'But most magic mirrors are designed for sunlight. Ours is designed for moonlight.'

The healthy skeptic looked a bit troubled. 'There must be an explanation for it,' he said, walking over to the mirror in his colleague's hands. 'There is an explanation for everything, after all. Perhaps there is a pattern of lines that is somehow in between the pattern at the back of the mirror and the shiny front.'

'Perhaps, but it would be difficult to make, if not impossible,' Brother Teh said.

Brother Sek nodded. 'Yes. It would be extremely tough to make. Let us list this as a mystery.' The skeptic continued, 'This device is very valuable and I think we should keep it in the monastery.'

'But it's ours,' said Mira. 'We need it.'

'Junior monks have no possessions,' said the skeptic, grabbing the mirror from Brother Teh's hands.

Marko leapt up, snatched the mirror from the small man's hands, and ran for the door. Mira scrambled to her feet and followed.

The healthy skeptic marched towards them—and by chance stepped on the sheet that Mira was using as a robe. It was pulled off.

'Whoops!' said Mira.

'A girl,' Brother Teh gasped.

'A girl,' several students said at once.

'A girl!' shouted the Healthy Skeptic angrily.

'Oh dear, dear me!' said Brother Teh. 'We may lose our right to become immortals.'

'This is an outrage,' the healthy skeptic bleated.

'Well, I think you're a load of sexists, the lot of you,' Mira said. But before she could continue, her brother grabbed her arm and pulled her away.

'Bye,' he said, 'and thanks—it's been very interesting.'

'After them!' said the skeptic.

***

By good fortune, the students who had arrived late had left the main door slightly ajar.

This meant that Mira and Marko could slip outside and then slam it shut—and no one would be able to open it, because the handle was on the outside.

But as Brother Teh had said earlier, the building was not very strongly built.

The two teachers and the students soon started pushing

down the door and it immediately started to crack.

After about two minutes, one of the young monks had bashed a big enough hole in the door so that he could reach through it and turn the handle. The monks poured out in a stream.

But by the time the monks were outside, the children had vanished.

The pursuers decided to fan out and search the area, many of them heading up to the mountains, believing the worst of mountain legends.

The healthy skeptic roared, 'We'll find you, devil woman!'

6

House of the Ancients

Trying not to breathe too loudly, the two children watched the young monks charge up the mountain paths in all directions from their shadowed hiding place.

Mira and Marko had decided, wisely as it turned out, that they would be highly unlikely to be able to outrun a group of strong young men who lived on a mountainside. The monks were used to going up and down steep slopes all the time, and would quickly out-pace a pair of young city kids used to buses and elevators for travelling the shortest of distances.

So the two children had stayed exactly where they were at the teaching house. The buildings were slightly raised off the ground, on a mixture of stones, bricks and stilts. The children had simply slipped into the crawl space under the building and sat in silence, watching their pursuers run off in hasty pursuit.

Once all the young monks were far away, well out of earshot, Mira said, 'What do we do now?'

Marko said, 'Don't know. Ask our leader. That's you, if I remember correctly.'

Mira pondered. 'I think we should go home.'

'But we haven't delivered the information we had to deliver. We're going to have to keep trying.'

'But how?'

'We need to go to the other house.'

He pointed to the building close to where the signpost lady had spoken to them. 'If people in building number one are not allowed to talk, and people in this building don't know what we're talking about, then it must be someone in the other building.'

Mira, meanwhile, was unnerved by the anger she had just generated. 'I think it's a crazy plan. I think we should run off and er ... re-group.' She wasn't quite sure what the phrase meant, but she had heard adults use it.

'What does that mean?'

'Umm ... It means disband and join again in a different formation.'

'But there's only two of us. How can we rejoin in a different formation?'

'I don't know. Look, it's just what people do when they're facing a difficult situation.'

They both turned to watch as the last figure in the

stream of angry monks, the rather unhealthy Brother Teh, disappeared from view.

'But which way would we go? They've gone in all directions. The last place they are going to look is back here. We're safer here than anywhere else.'

She considered this. 'I want to go home. I don't feel safe here.'

'You're supposed to be the boss, right? You're supposed to be leading us to get this job done.'

'I suppose so. Let's get finished soon, then. We better go home as soon as we have delivered our message. Whoever we are looking for MUST be in that building, right?'

***

A few minutes later, Mira had become a boy again, this time with her robe tightly tucked in and tied on, and they were knocking on the door of the middle house. This time there were no handles on the outside of the door, so they must be on the inside.

'Yes?' said an old man's voice.

'Can you open the door?' Marko asked.

'Who are you?'

'We're two students.'

'Both boys,' Mira added.

'We are not the vandals that have been seen around,' Marko said.

'Yeah, we are tourists, visitors from another place. You should be welcoming towards us, because two of you are going to be made immortals, right?'

'You know about that?'

'We do.'

'Do you know which two? What have you heard? Are you messengers from some sort of committee?'

Mira thought for a moment. 'No, we're not messengers. And we don't know which two of you are going to be made immortals. But it could be you. Being kind to travellers would definitely win you some points. If someone takes an opinion poll, we would definitely vote for you.'

The door opened a crack. When the elderly man peeked out and saw how young the visitors were, he opened it fully. 'Come in.'

The man was thin and bald, with a spotty head.

'We have a message to deliver,' Mira said. 'We just want to see if it means anything to you or one of your colleagues.' She nudged her brother.

He pulled out the book of poetry and turned to the handwritten note. 'It says that the answer to your question is 'Lady Annee and the Record of Ancient Mirrors'.'

The old man blinked.

Mira was immediately excited. Did his reaction mean that

this was the right guy? 'So that message means something to you?'

'No,' the old man said, shaking his head. 'It makes no sense at all, which is very strange, because this is the house of the old, and we're supposed to know everything and everyone around here. Never heard of anyone called Annee.'

Mira was crestfallen.

Marko sighed. 'There's no one here called Annee or anything similar? Anu or Anand or Anna?' he asked.

'There are no women here at all, except the talking signpost, a lady who stands outside to guide travellers, so there can't be anyone named Annee, which sounds like a girl's name to me. And I have heard of the Record of Ancient Mirrors, but we don't have a copy of that here, as far as I know. It's probably in the capital city in a museum. It sounds like that sort of book. But you could ask at the main house.'

'But no one's allowed to talk there. So we can't ask anything and expect an answer.'

'That's true. What about the training house? They're allowed to talk there.'

Marko said, 'We already tried that. No good. Is there anyone else here, in this building? We've been told to deliver that message to someone, and we kinda think it might be meant for someone here.'

'Who are you supposed to deliver the message to? What name?'

'Not sure,' the boy admitted. 'Just to someone here on Cold Mountain.'

'Hard to deliver a message if you don't have a name to deliver it to.'

'Yes, we know.'

Mira said, 'Is there anyone else here other than you?' She hoped there would be someone younger and sharper who might be a bit more helpful.

'Let me take you to my colleague,' the elderly man said. 'See if he knows something.'

'Is he as old as you are?'

'No, certainly not,' said the old man. 'He's much older.'

***

'We're all very careful these days,' said a tiny ancient man who was being measured by a gold foil salesman. 'There was a prophecy last year that the two top monks at this monastery would live forever, so we've been very careful ever since. It's a great honour, obviously, so we have to respect it.'

Marko raised his hand to ask a question. 'What do you mean live forever? Like, not die, ever? Just get older and older and older for ever and ever?'

The aged man, who had been introduced to them as The

Ancient of Days, shrugged. 'Well, the term 'living forever' can have two meanings. One is the literal one—the monks will keep on living eternally, joining the ranks of the immortals, no longer bound by the limits of human flesh. The other is the figurative one—the monks will create a great teaching or fine book or excellent example which will mean their names will be celebrated forever. Some people say that the two meanings are both the same thing.'

Mira asked, 'Who are the two top monks? They must be pleased. Do you think it's you two? Like, what's the betting?'

Both of the old men laughed. The younger one blushed. The ancient one said, 'Who knows? That's the whole point. That's why we are all being so careful. You see, it is impossible to tell who the top two monks are. The ones who are leaders? The ones who are wisest? The ones who are oldest? The ones who are most spiritual? The ones who have the best mixture of various qualities? It is impossible to tell.'

'When do you find out who it is?'

'Destiny does not supply advance dates of great happenings. So we are all being very careful. Doing our best to make sure there is no bad behaviour, no drunkenness, no breaking of rules, no women on the premises, that sort of thing.'

Marko was intrigued. 'I guess life is quite good with no girls. I hope I live in a house with no girls when I grow up.'

Mira gave him a dig with her elbow.

'Ow!'

'That's not nice,' she whispered out of the side of her mouth, before turning back to the old man at the desk. 'The important question is this. Is there anyone else in this building we can give our message to? We have to deliver it today. Tonight,' she added, noticing the sun setting out of the old man's window.

The two men shook their heads.

'So you can't help us?'

The ancient monk held up one gnarled finger. 'We can't help you deliver your message. But we can help you with a piece of advice.'

'Go on then,' said Mira, standing up, already impatient to leave. She was painfully aware that the young men who had run off up the mountain would eventually be on their way down again.

The old man said, 'The advice is this. You are not very talented at pretending to be a boy, young lady. If I were you, I would do it as little as possible.'

Mira blushed. 'I'm not a girl,' she stammered. 'I'm just a boy with a girly face.'

'A ... a ... a woman?' asked the other monk, surprised.

The ancient one laughed. 'You were fooled? Why am I not surprised?'

Marko and Miranda ran out of the room. 'Gotta go! Bye.' While the ancient monk cackled, the younger man called for help. 'There's a woman on the premises. Quick! Come!'

'At least we can outrun these old folks,' said Mira, as they raced towards the trees.

7

Companions of Conspiracy

As they reached the cover of trees off the main path—they had scrambled up an overgrown hill with great difficulty for a good five minutes—Mira was becoming seriously worried. There were now two groups of people who were angry with her and actively trying to seek her out to inflict some sort of punishment on her. They needed to complete their mission quickly and leave.

Yet, what could they do? They sat behind a bush, breathing deeply and getting their strength back.

Then they heard a woman's voice.

'Lost? Or hiding?'

Mira turned to see the talking signpost standing behind them. She must have been very light on her feet to get this close without them hearing her.

'Er ... we decided to get off the path and take some rest,' Mira said.

Marko said, 'We couldn't find the right person to give our

message to. And people are a bit angry with us.'

The Mobile Signpost smiled and looked directly at Mira. 'You remind me of myself when I was young. I was always in trouble, finding myself in places where I was not supposed to be. And see where I ended up. I could have done worse, I guess.'

Mira said, 'We really, really want to just deliver our message and then disappear. Are there any other people living around here? Anyone at all?'

The woman scratched her chin. 'There are always travellers passing by, but living here? Other than one or two eccentrics, there's only the monastery-temple complex.'

Marko said, 'But we have a message to deliver to someone. We tried the training house, like you suggested, and the retired monks' home, and the person we're looking for isn't there. People can't talk at the main monastery building, so it can't be anyone there.'

'But do you have no name? That makes it difficult.'

'There must be someone else living around here.'

'No. Except for the occasional crazy person who loses his brain and tries to live on the mountain, the temple complex is all there is.'

Mira was looking behind her. There was a wonderful smell coming from somewhere. Was it fried onions?

'I'm so sorry, but I don't think I can help you,' the signpost said.

'I wonder if we are on the wrong mountain or in the wrong country,' Marko said to his sister, although she was no longer paying attention to him.

'Mmm ... what *is* that smell? I am *so* hungry,' she said, inhaling deeply through her nose.

The woman smiled. 'It's cooking time at the main monastery. Wait—that might be your answer. The one person who is allowed to speak at the main building is the cook. Have you asked him?'

She pointed to a small hut at the back of the main complex which had steam or smoke coming out of several windows, and a chimney.

'The cookhouse,' said Mira. 'Maybe the cook can give us a snack. I'm starving.'

'Good luck!' the woman called out, but the children were already gone.

A minute later, the pair were in the messy, heat-filled hut. The cook turned out to be a single, rather harassed-looking individual with shaggy hair who was dealing with several steaming pots at once on a large but primitive wood-fired stove. He seemed to be mumbling to himself, but in no language they could recognise.

'Can you talk?' Marko asked.

'No,' said the cook.

'But you just did.'

'I can talk but not now because I'm too busy. Work now, talk later.'

Marko said, 'We just want some information, like where we are. Is this the mountain of poems?'

He turned and glared at him.

'What?'

'The mountain of poems. The cold mountain.'

The man looked puzzled. Then he gave them a short half-smile.

'Look, why don't you help me in the kitchen? It's nearly time for the meal and I could do with some extra hands. The monks are hosting a party of their brothers from a monastery in the next valley. Then, afterwards, we'll talk. One hour of work, ten minutes of talk. That's the deal, take it or leave it.'

Mira said, 'Can we get some lunch too? I haven't eaten for hours.'

He introduced himself as Shi-De, master of cookery, and gave them each a piece of flatbread. 'Have these for now—they will give you some energy. After the monks have been fed, we'll eat something ourselves. Leftovers.'

'Will there be any leftovers?'

'If we cook enough now, we can make sure there'll be plenty.'

***

They worked hard for the next hour, cooking food, pouring it into large bowls, and then cooking more food—before carrying it all out to the main hall, where more than 100 monks were waiting to be fed. It was strange to be in a room with so many people and to hear no conversation at all.

But that didn't mean it was silent. Somehow, because of the lack of human voices, the other little noises in the room all seemed to be unnaturally loud. People were coughing and burping and scraping their chairs around, and the whole thing seemed to add up to a surprisingly loud hum of background noise. The monks even managed, somehow, to make silent jokes to each other using only hands and eyes—you could tell, because there was occasionally a snort or a grunt or a chuckle or a murmur of assent.

Once all the food was placed onto the long tables and everyone was seated, there was a minute of silence as the monks gave thanks for their meal.

They bowed their heads simultaneously, without a signal, and all looked up two minutes later at the same time, again with no audible sign.

But just as the men were reaching for the food, a tall, thin monk at the end of the room, his face half hidden by a floppy hood, looked at his food and said, quite loudly, 'YUM YUM!'

Everyone immediately stopped and stared at him. He turned to look around the room, a grin on his face.

There was a scraping of chairs as several people rose to their feet to go and confront the man who had spoken.

'Uh-oh,' he said in a theatrically loud voice, and leapt to his feet. He picked up his dinner plate and started to leave.

Clearly, he was an intruder. The robe he was in appeared to have been thrown on over his normal clothes, and was ill-fitting, the back of it trailing on the floor.

Mira watched with her hand over her mouth. Who was this guy? An intruder? Or was this a case of mutiny?

The monks remained silent, although there was a definite unease in the air as they stared at the misbehaving man.

One monk grabbed the man's cloak and it fell away into his hand. Underneath, the person was wearing a curious costume. It was a brown, striped garment, and parts of it were stiff, while other parts moved, making a sound like paper rustling. It looked like it had been made of tree bark.

'Goodbye, my friends, and thanks for the delicious dinner,' said the interloper, racing out of reach. He jumped out of the monastery window, his steaming bowl still in his hands.

Marko turned and saw that Shi-De was grinning. But as soon as the cook realised he was being watched, his expression changed to one of disapproval.

Several of the monks were making grumbling noises, and Shi-De joined in too with a low grumble. Then he spoke out loud. 'I will lock the back gates, make sure he doesn't get back in.'

But as the cook walked back to the kitchen, Marko saw that he was laughing quietly.

***

Later, the cook and the two children sat at a small table in the cramped kitchen, eating and drinking leftovers from the monks' meal. There was plenty of food and it tasted great.

'Who was that guy?' Mira asked. 'That guy who sneaked in and stole a meal? He was funny.'

Shi-De smiled at the memory, but lowered his voice when he spoke. 'That, my friends, was the man with no name.'

'But why was he dressed like a monk?'

'He wanted to eat, just like you want to eat. It's cold, it's windy. We all need to have something warm and filling in our tummies. And you must admit I'm a pretty good cook.'

'You are. I don't usually eat vegetables, but yours are okay,' the girl said.

'Okay?'

'Pretty good, in fact.'

Marko, his mouth full of steamed vegetables, said, 'So, that guy wants to eat the monks' food?'

'That's right. But it's really reserved for the monks and the temple workers. He hasn't taken the right vows or anything, so he's not really entitled to it. A bit cheeky.'

'I'll say,' the boy agreed. 'Why doesn't he become a monk, if he wants to eat with the monks?'

'He says he's on an important mission.'

'Oh. What is it?'

'Well, that's the problem. Nobody knows what this mission is, except him. And he's forgotten.'

Mira looked up. 'If it's important, how come he's forgotten?'

Marko said, 'He sounds crazy. He looks crazy too.'

His sister said, 'Does anyone believe him?'

Shi-De nodded. 'Yes. He has one friend.'

'Who?'

'Me. I believe him. The way he behaves, his manner, his look: it is that of a nobleman. I think he was a nobleman who somehow lost his mind—maybe through sickness or an accident or something. Who knows what happened? And he has ended up here. Perhaps he was on his way to somewhere.'

Mira said, 'And he doesn't have a name? Has he forgotten that too?'

'No name. All forgotten.'

They ate for a while in silence, and then Marko asked, 'Why does he hang out around here? Shouldn't he go searching for where he's supposed to be?'

Shi-De mopped the sauce off his plate with a piece of bread and popped it into his mouth before replying, 'That's the problem. He is convinced that this is where he is supposed to be. So he won't leave. Whatever he is looking for, it's here. The answer to the mystery that drives him is somewhere right here on this mountain.'

The boy's brow crinkled. 'How do you know so much about him?'

Shi-De smiled. It was a conspiratorial smirk. 'He and I have a shared interest. A shared love, you could say.'

'A girlfriend?' This was Mira.

'No. But equally difficult and time-consuming. A passion. A pastime.'

'A game?'

'No. A skill. An art. A form of magic, created with a pen. You would probably call it poetry.'

'You both write poems!'

Shi-De gave a little bow.

'Really?' Marko asked. 'Did you write the poems on the rocks?'

'No. I prefer to write on paper, the traditional way. Our eccentric friend writes on every surface that will take a line from his pen—rocks, trees, walls, anything.'

Mira's eyes widened. 'The monks told us about two vandals in the upper parts of the mountain. Are they ...?'

Shi-De nodded. 'Our eccentric friend and myself, yes. The monks don't know that I'm his buddy—well, some of them probably suspect it by now. But I live in a cave up on the northwestern side of the hill, and our friend in the tree-bark clothing lives next door. In fact, it was he who showed me the cave. Very resourceful man.'

Mira finished her last piece of bread and stood up, pushing the stool away from her with the back of her legs.

'Look, it's nice talking to you and all that, but we are on an urgent mission and it's getting dark. We have a message to deliver, and we're hoping that someone here might know who we should talk to.'

Her brother stood up too. 'Do you know the names of the people around here, maybe around the foothills of the mountain?

'We're looking for someone who needs information about a friend or family member named Annee.'

Shi-De shook his head. 'Names? I just told you, I don't even know the name of my best friend.'

Mira was puzzled. 'What do you call him? The guy in the

tree-bark suit? I mean, when you refer to him, what do you say? Do you just say, 'that guy'?'

Shi-De stood up. 'He is getting quite well-known, not just because of his eccentricity. He is also a rather fine poet, despite his strange obsessions. So people refer to him by his address, which is, of course, this large lump of rock. They call him Cold Mountain, which is Han Shan in the local language.'

The two children looked at each other.

'Cold Mountain!' Marko repeated, not believing what he had just heard.

Mira grabbed Shi-De's arm. 'His name is Cold Mountain?'

Shi-De was clearly intrigued by their reaction. It indicated that their earlier reference to his friend's nickname was no random event.

The two children looked at each other and grinned.

'Paydirt!' said Mira.

She sat down again.

She snapped her fingers to indicate to her brother that he should get his book out.

'I think we have some information for him. It might be the information he's looking for—whatever it is that he has forgotten. It's right here.'

Marko took out his poetry book and turned to the opening pages.

8

History & Her story

It was a long walk up the winding mountain path to the cave, but it was surprisingly pleasant. When you're stuffed with good food, a bit of gentle exercise makes you feel good.

During the conversation in the monastery kitchen, the two children had explained to Shi-De that they had been given a specific assignment today, without going into details about where they had come from. 'Our grandfather gave us a message that we were to come here and deliver this message.'

'But it means nothing to me,' said the cook. 'I don't think it will mean anything to Cold Mountain, either. Can I see it again?'

Marko read it out loud. 'Urgent! Go to the great mountain of poems tonight and tell Cold Mountain that the answer to the question is "Lady Annee and The Record of Ancient Mirrors".'

Mira said, 'This must be something to do with the mission that your friend ... what did you call him?'

'Hanshan.'

'... that Hanshan was on before he lost his mind or whatever.'

Shi-De agreed. 'It's possible. It all seems very strange—but it can do no harm to try. Who is Annee?'

Marko said, 'We don't know. We haven't heard that name before.'

Mira said, 'But let's take this to the crazy guy anyway. Just in case. It must be for him—unless there are lots of people around here called Cold Mountain.'

Shi-De shook his head. 'No others, I'm sure.'

They walked for another 20 minutes in companionable silence, through a beautiful tree-lined path that wound round the mountain—and then left the main trail to follow a path that appeared to be hidden, weaving between rocks and trees.

'I like poetry,' said Marko, brushing branches aside. 'I'm reading a book of poetry at the moment.'

'Poetry's all very well,' Mira put in sourly. 'But it doesn't actually DO anything. I prefer prose, where people tell you stories or inform you about real achievements by real people talking about interesting stuff. Like game design.'

'Oh, but prose comes out of poetry,' said Shi-De. 'And so do stories.'

The cheerful cook became rather serious as he slipped into lecture mode.

'Let me tell you how it works. For years, and I mean thousands of years, all stories were told out loud, and repeated down the generations.'

'People had to remember how they went, since writing had not been invented yet. So stories used sentences filled with special things that helped you memorise them—rhyme and rhythm and alliteration and all the things that make a sentence special. In other words, they were poems.'

'We study poems at school. They are kind of boring,' said Mira.

'Well, you obviously don't study the great poets,' the cook said. 'Anyway, so the first stories were not prose but poetry. By having these special elements, they were easy to remember.'

Mira said, 'You guys can enjoy your poetry. I've got a book on games which I can read. That will be more my kind of thing.'

She took her book of games out of her pocket and started reading it with some difficulty as they strolled along the hidden path.

Shi-De continued with his lecture. 'If we look at the earliest writings, we will find that they are very practical pieces of text: notes on accounts, dates of battles and victories, records of when kings and emperors took the throne or left it. But then came the poets. One of the greatest of ancient books is one called The Classic of Poetry, written hundreds of years ago—one of the first great books of mankind. It's a collection of poems.'

'Are they good poems?' Marko asked. 'Any funny ones? I like funny ones best.'

'There are lots of great poems in it—funny, sad, of every style. But this is the interesting bit. The warrior kings and noblemen wrote their records of battles won, and how many sheep they had, or on what date they got what job. But poets, many of them women, wrote about something quite different. They wrote about ordinary life, and their hopes and fears. The soldiers scoffed at them. They thought that their own writings, records of how many sheep they had, were valuable documents. But a piece of writing about feelings—what use was it?'

This was interesting, so Mira couldn't help but listen.

Shi-De continued with a quick glance at the girl. 'And then, when years and centuries passed, people discovered something. The record of how many sheep you had, or when the rulers of the district travelled from A to B were of very little interest to anyone except historians. On the other hand, the poems that the women had written—little gems which recreated the hopes and fears of ordinary people—these turned out to be much more valuable. When you read them, you can actually feel yourself transported back hundreds of years, and you can share the deepest feelings of someone who lived in those olden days. That is the magic of poetry.'

Mira had to interrupt. 'So you're saying what the women wrote was more important than what the men wrote?'

'Well, it's not a battle between the sexes,' Shi-De said. 'But it is definitely true that poetry, which seems rather unimportant in a community which is shaped by battles and feuds between warlords, turned out in the long run to be the most powerful way of really learning about the past.'

The cook suddenly stopped moving. He dropped to his knees and signalled for the children to do the same. They were silent. It appeared that there was danger nearby.

Then they could hear rustling sounds.

Someone was coming towards them through the undergrowth.

'Stay down,' whispered Shi-De. 'Let me check who it is.'

The two children crouched down while the shaggy-haired poet slowly lifted his head to look over the top of a gorse bush.

He dropped down to his knees again. 'We need to run. Quick.'

The three of them scampered away.

Marko noticed that Shi-De was grinning again, and he was laughing like crazy by the time they were several hundred metres away from the visitor.

'What's so funny?' Mira gasped, as they stepped off the path and hid behind a large fallen log.

'That man,' said Shi-De.

'Isn't he dangerous?' asked Marko, still speaking in a whisper.

Shi-De shook his head. 'Not at all. He is our most enthusiastic follower.'

'What do you mean? You mean he's the leader of your fan club?'

'He loves our work. He collects it, especially Hanshan's. He copies it off the rocks and trees. When Hanshan wrote a poem on a house wall, he tried to buy the wall.'

Mira was annoyed. 'So why are we running from him?'

'Poets need to maintain an air of mystery,' Shi-De said. 'It's very important not to reveal too much of yourself to your followers.'

As they resumed their walk, taking a different path, Shi-De explained that the man's named was Lu Jiuyin, and he was governor of Tai Prefecture. He had become a keen collector of Hanshan's writings.

'He met Hanshan and me at the kitchen of Guoqing Temple for the first time about a year ago. He praised us to the skies, but we laughed and nipped out the back door. A few days later, he turned up on the mountain again and attempted to give us clothing and provide housing for us—proper houses in the town, paid for by the government.'

'What did you do?' Mira asked. 'Don't you want a free house?'

'We vanished into thin air. We can do that sort of thing, you know.'

'Like magic?' asked Mira, skeptically. 'I'd like to see that.'

'No,' the cook said. 'Not magic, but trickery. We have ways of slipping into cave openings that no one else can see. Several times he follows our tracks and then they completely disappear. He thinks we have superhuman powers.'

Mira laughed. 'It seems odd for celebrities to avoid their fans.'

Shi-De said, 'The more we avoid him, the more he pursues us. It's odd, but the more mysterious we become, the more frantically he searches for us. He says he is going to put us in the history books.'

9

Frightening Followers

On the mountain path in the evening gloom, government official Lu Jiuyin heard something behind him. He stopped and turned. A sharp, gruff voice, masculine and deep, snarled at him.

'You. You there, stop. Come here.'

Lu's mouth fell open.

Standing in the clearing on the mountainside were two people dressed in outlandish clothing—a man with heavy but ornate armour, clearly a soldier of some sort, and a woman in silk finery of exquisite design, who looked like a young queen. She was tall and breathtakingly beautiful.

The soldier was now marching towards him. 'You. I want to speak to you.'

Lu stood and waited for the soldier, deeming it wise to remain polite and resist his urge to turn and flee.

'We need information.'

The government official, watching them approach,

decided that the two newcomers must be regal visitors from a foreign land, and thus should be treated with careful respect. Lu bowed twice, and then addressed his comments to the queenly woman, who was, by this time, also stepping towards him.

'My name is Lu,' he said, with a half-bow. 'I am the governor of Tai Prefecture. I will be happy to provide you with any assistance I can. I can give you a tour of the district or introduce you to the work of our finest poets.'

The soldier looked around. 'Where are we? Is this Guoqing temple, Tiantai mountain?'

'It is. We are on the southern slope, about a quarter of the way up. Are you looking for a particular place? The monastery?'

The man did not answer, but turned to the woman.

She said, 'Who lives in this place?' Her voice was musical and refined, as beautiful as the rest of her.

Lu pulled at his fine moustaches. 'Not many people. We have the monastery, a short walk from here. Nothing else.'

'That is the only building?'

'Well, it consists of three structures, but yes, that's the only building in this district.'

'We seek this man.' She pulled Annee's locket out of her pocket and opened it to show a small image of Duke Anchee Daakan Lee Daaken Lee III.

Lu peered at it. 'There are many men like that here—the monastery is full of men, and some are of that age. But none who dress like that.' The character in the image was as curiously dressed as the newcomers, in garments that were tight on the limbs, but flowing around the shoulders.

The queenly woman, who he noticed had not introduced herself, looked exasperated. 'Are there no people here except for the monks?'

'None at all. Except for a few vagabonds on the hills—including two who write surprisingly good poetry, if you are interested in the literary arts. Well worth a visit.'

The soldier spat. 'Let's go.' He turned around.

The woman put up one hand to signal that he should pause. 'No, wait. What do you mean poetry?'

Lu said, 'Exactly what I said. In addition to the monastery, this mountain is also the home of two poets, who live humbly in caves in the upper reaches. You can see the writing of one of them inscribed on the very rocks.'

Something occurred to him. The government official spoke slowly as his mind started to race. Hanshan the poet was of a curious bearing, noble, oddly dressed, and often speaking and behaving in a strange manner, as if he was from a distant land, just like these two. 'Show me the image again,' he said.

This time, he looked at it for long, trying to remove the odd finery in the image and replace it with Hanshan's curious tree-bark hat and tunic.

The woman said, 'You have seen this man?'

'I guarantee nothing. But it is possible that the man you seek is one of the poets of whom I speak. The man is extremely eccentric, but I believe he is of noble breeding.'

'What is the man's name?'

'He has no name. Or none that he will reveal to us. He claims to have ... forgotten it.'

The woman's eyes lit up. 'He has forgotten it! Is he an outsider? Was he not born here?' She turned to the soldier. 'Kutter said that the portal would destroy his mind.'

Governor Lu continued, 'He was not born here. He has been here a year or so only.'

The woman looked at the soldier and then back at the official. 'This man with no name: what does he do? Other than write poetry?'

Lu considered the question. 'He says he is on a mission, but he has forgotten what it is. It sounds strange, I know, but you have to make allowances for the poetic mind. It is not unusual for poets to be like this.'

'Take us to him.'

Lu did not move. 'It is not as simple as that,' he said. 'I am a government official. I have performed many formal duties, including the greeting of visitors from other nations, and the escorting of such persons on tours. The first thing we need to do is to receive a token of goodwill from you—so that we can be assured that you mean us no harm.'

The soldier spoke. 'What do you mean by "a token of goodwill"?'

'A mark of friendship. It does not need to be a valuable gift. It could simply be a letter from your king, or a piece of art from your finest artist, or a written agreement.'

The soldier pulled out his sword. It had clearly been sharpened to a razor's edge, and polished until it shone. This was unmistakably a man who came from a community that treasured weapons. 'See this?' the soldier asked. 'This is what I call a piece of art. And if you do not take us to this poet friend of yours right now, you will receive this piece of art in a way that you may not like.'

Lu swallowed but showed no other physical response. 'I see. Fine. Follow me.'

As he led them up the sloping path, Lu gave them a string of gentle warnings. 'He may not see you, you know. He and his partner are very private men. They also have some odd powers which help them avoid visitors.'

The woman was interested. 'What odd powers?'

'Well, for a start, they know the caves that bedevil this hillside very well. One moment you are following them, and then—poof! They have vanished. Just disappeared into thin air. It has happened to me far too often.'

***

Marko Lee sat in the cave at Shi-De's feet, hearing the laughing cook tell stories about poets and poetry.

Then a small bell rang, the gentlest of tinkling sounds.

'Someone is approaching,' the cook said, suddenly alert. 'Must be that Lu again.'

'Who's pulling the bell?' Marko asked. 'Do you have a guard out there standing watch?'

'No. Merely some safety devices. Amazing what you can do with strings of creeping vines, you know. Now be quiet for a moment.'

Shi-Di stepped to the mouth of the cave and then pulled a series of strings made from knotted plant fibres. Watching from the top, the children could see bushes moving.

'I am covering up the path we used, and uncovering one which leads right past us,' said Shi-De in a whisper.

After he had finished disguising the paths, the cook climbed up a rocky outcrop above the cave entrance. 'Just taking a look,' he told them.

A few seconds later, his brow furrowed.

'What is it?' Mira asked in a whisper from below the rock.

'I have no idea. I was expecting Official Lu again, but he seems to have brought two friends with him. One appears to be a fine noblewoman, perhaps a princess or a queen, and the other is surely her bodyguard: a soldier, heavily armed, and with a great sword.'

'Let me see,' Mira said, scrambling up. 'Maybe that's Annee.'

Seconds later, the girl was on the rock too—and half a minute later, she had been joined by her brother. 'There's no room up here for three of us,' she whined.

'There is if you don't push.'

'You're the one who's pushing.'

'Only to stop you pushing me off.'

She turned to see if she could spot the people the cook was talking about. 'Where? I can't see anyone.'

Shi-De pointed to some figures winding their way up the mountain.

'Oh, there. Right. I see what you mean. She *is* a princess. Looks like one, anyway. Wow, she's beautiful.'

She turned to look at her brother. 'I'll bet you anything you like that that's the Annee who's mentioned in the message. It's gotta be her.'

Marko shrugged. 'I guess it could be.'

'It must be. You know Hanshan, the 'Cold Mountain' guy? I reckon he's a prince who has lost his memory. And our job is to remind him that he is supposed to be looking for princess Annee—and here she is.'

'It just says Annee, not princess Annee.'

'Look at her, she's clearly a princess. And she's *looking* for her prince.'

'How do you know she's looking for her prince?'

'Because she's a princess. That's what princesses do, look for their princes. Not that a princess needs a prince,' she added hurriedly. 'Princesses can do fine without princes, if they want to. But they can have them if they want them.'

'I think we should be careful,' said Shi-De. 'We don't know anything about these people and they are dressed strangely. Like you two.' He gave them a suspicious glance.

But Mira had made her decision. She stood up on the rock and shouted.

'Annee! We're here! Up here! Come this way.'

The cook winced.

'Sorry,' Marko said to Shi-De, whose eyes were popping. 'She's always like this. I have to put up with this every day.'

***

A few minutes later, the two groups were suspiciously eyeing each other outside Shi-De's cave.

'Why did you call me Annee?' the woman asked.

'You're not Annee?'

'I'm Lady Anastasia, her sister. But I want to know where you got Annee's name. From someone you met on this mountain?'

'No. We were given it by our grandfather,' Mira said. 'You see, there's a guy who lost his mind on this mountain, and he's forgotten some important things. One of them is the name of his friend, Annee. Is Annee his wife?'

'No,' said the woman. 'I am his wife. Lady Annee is my sister. You can call me ma'am.'

Marko asked, 'What happened, please, ma'am? How did he forget everything? Was he in an accident?'

The regal woman nodded. 'Yes. He was in a terrible, terrible accident—it's a matter of good fortune that he survived at all. But clearly his mind was deeply damaged in the accident. It's exactly what we expected.'

'So are you going to take him home?'

She gave the children a warm, comforting smile. 'Yes. Just tell me where he is and we will take him back to the palace. He needs care.'

Marko said, 'And then you'll all live happily ever after, right? I read this in so many books. The whole fairy tale thing.'

'I knew it,' said Mira. 'You're a princess and he is a prince, right?'

Lady Anastasia nodded. 'You can think of us like that if you like. His rank is actually Duke, and I am a Lady, but we will eventually rule over our land when we return.'

She turned to Shi-De. 'Now you need to tell us where to find him.'

From a pouch attached to her belt, she pulled out a ring with a large glassy stone on top. It didn't sparkle like a diamond, but had a dull light of several colours, like a midnight rainbow.

'Hold this in your hands,' she ordered, looking at the cook.

Shi-De took hold of the curious object and admired it.

'It is a stone that enables me to tell whether you are lying. If you are telling the truth, it will shine with blue light. If not, it will turn red. Now, where can I find the man with no name?'

Shi-De pointed to the right.

'He is at the foot of the mountain, in a boat on the river.'

The object in his hands turned red. 'Ow!' he said, and tried to drop it. But he couldn't shake it off.

'Ow! Ow! It's stuck! It's stuck to me. And it's burning me.'

But the red glow disappeared as he spoke, and a blue shimmer reappeared.

Lady Anastasia said, 'Speak the truth and it will remain

cool, and glow blue but will do you no harm. Tell me a lie and it will hurt you.'

Shi-De gulped. He stared at the ring in his hands, suddenly terrified of it.

Anastasia gave him an icy smile. 'It would be better if you just told the truth straight away. This is a wonderful tool that saves me so much time.'

The cook nodded. 'At this time he is in the Chess Pavilion. That's where he goes in the evenings because he likes the light there. It's on top of the mountain. In the evenings, there are no visitors there.

The stone continued to glow blue.

'How do we get there?'

'You can reach the Chess Pavilion by following this path to the right. When you get to three pine trees, you look slightly downhill on your left, and you will see a lightly trodden path sloping upwards. That's the way to go. You travel along it for several minutes until you see it fork.'

The crystal continued to shine.

Government Official Lu interrupted. 'Yes, my lady, this is the truth. I know the three pines of which he speaks, and also of the fork in the path further along.'

Which fork should we take—the left or the right?'

'Neither. Look uphill and you will see a third choice—this

one is well-hidden. Move the thornberry bushes aside and look for animal tracks. It is this third track that you must take. Follow it as it winds once to the right, then to the left, and then up a stone staircase in the stone. The staircase leads to High Cave. At the back of High Cave are the steps to the Chess Pavilion.'

Again, the woman, who was clearly of a suspicious nature, turned to look at the glowing stone. It remained blue.

'He and your crystal are correct, I believe,' said government official Lu.

Shi-De looked aggrieved. 'You are so suspicious! This is unfair. I am from the monastery. Of course I tell the truth.'

'Are you a monk?' Anastasia asked.

Lu said, 'He is the cook at the monastery.'

'So you are no monk.'

The government official stepped over to Shi-De. 'Madam, he is something even greater than a monk. He is a poet.'

'Yes, yes,' the woman said dismissively. 'Now we must go. Lead us.'

Lu led the way on the path to the Chess Pavilion, with Lady Anastasia and the soldier close behind.

***

When they were out of hearing range, Marko said, 'They were not nice people.'

Mira agreed. 'Princesses are supposed to be nice. I can't understand why she is so grumpy. Maybe I shouldn't have called her over.'

Shi-De folded his arms. 'Oh, *now* you have finally worked that out.'

Mira said, 'And maybe you shouldn't have told her where to find Hanshan.'

'Is that where he really is?' Marko asked.

Shi-De nodded. 'Oh yes, I was telling the truth. Hanshan really is in the Chess Pavilion, if I know him.'

Mira said, 'Perhaps we ought to follow them. Maybe they mean to do him some harm? Besides, we still haven't delivered our message. We have to do that before they take him away.'

Shi-De smiled. 'Oh, yes, we should definitely join Hanshan at High Cave.'

Marko stepped towards the path. But he looked behind him to see that Shi-De had not moved.

'Let's go then,' said Mira, always impatient. 'We need to catch up with them.'

Shi-De turned to go back to his cave.

'Where are you going? We need to set off.'

'Yes.'

'So they went that way,' Marko said, pointing to the distance.

'Yes.'

'But you're going back into your cave.'

'Yes.'

'Aren't you coming?'

'I am. But I just thought we might as well take the shortcut. I sent them the long way round. It *is* the way to the cave, so I told the truth, as far as the stone is concerned—but it's the long way. You can get there much faster if you take a shortcut through the cave system.'

He began to laugh again, that low, slightly crazy laugh of his.

10

Moonlit Magic

They scrambled through a system of winding tunnels, following a flame torch held aloft by Shi-De. At first it was a difficult journey. It was hard to get used to the combination of darkness and a waving flame. But after a few minutes, their eyes adjusted to the situation.

By that time, they kept their gaze on a moving ring of light around Shi-De as he sprinted towards his friend. The children found that as long as they kept him directly in front of them, they could move as fast as he could, without grazing their knees or elbows on the uneven sides of the cavern.

They ran steadily for seven or eight minutes, and then Shi-De slowed down. They must be nearly there.

Then he stopped. Mira, who was in a daze, bumped into the cook, and then Marko bumped into her. 'Sorry,' the two youngsters whispered. There was a curious soft, silver light in front of them. Night had fallen.

'We're too late,' Shi-De whispered. 'They are already

here. On the outside, too, there are shortcuts, and Lu must have taken them through those.'

Marko stared over the cook's shoulder and saw a large open-walled room on top of a mountain, lit with clear gray-white moonlight. The light flickered as wisps of cloud drifted in front of the moon.

In the middle was a tall, thin figure, seated on a bench, reading a book. It was the man in the tree-bark clothes who had caused such a commotion in the monks' dining hall.

He was looking up at visitors who had just arrived from an opposite entrance.

'Anchee,' Lady Anastasia said. She was clearly excited to see him again—her voice was suddenly high and breathy. 'The gods be praised. We have found you. After so long.'

Behind her, Harshender stepped into the room and folded his arms.

Hanshan stood up. He looked puzzled, his head tilted slightly to one side.

'Do I know you?' he asked.

'You know me,' Lady Anastasia said. 'I am your wife. My name is Anastasia. You have had a terrible, terrible accident, and lost your memory. We have been looking for you for years. Thank God you're safe.'

She took a step towards him.

But he stepped away.

'You know me, it seems. But do I know you?'

'I am your wife. Of course I know you. I know your name and I know what you are looking for. You have been seeking something for years, am I not right?'

Hanshan nodded, but was still suspicious of her, keeping his distance. 'I have spent years trying to recover something. You are right, although I have not been able to find it, or even learn what it is. Nor have I found any clues in my surroundings.'

Lady Anastasia took another step towards him. This time he did not back away from her.

'Your name is Duke Anchee Daakan Lee Daakan Lee III,' she said. 'You had an accident. You lost your memory. You wandered away from where you were supposed to be. You came here.'

He suddenly started pacing around the chamber. 'No, this seems wrong. I am in the right place. I feel I am in the right place. But you're right, I am seeking something. Indeed, I am looking for two things. One is a name—a name I cannot remember. A girl's name. And the second is an object. But that too I have forgotten.'

The woman gave him the same warm, deceptive smile that she had earlier given Shi-De and the youngsters. 'I know exactly what you are looking for. The girl's name you seek is mine: Anastasia. I am your wife.'

'And the object I seek?'

Lady Anastasia did not reply. She did not have a ready answer to the question.

At that point, Miranda Lee ran into the chamber.

'Stop,' said Shi-De.

But it was too late. Mira ran between Cold Mountain and Lady Anastasia. Marko followed close behind. 'She's wrong. She's trying to fool you,' Mira said. 'The name you are looking for is Annee.'

'I can spell it for you if you like,' added Marko helpfully, holding up his book.

Hanshan looked at the two youngsters and then at his friend, who was now standing behind them. 'Shi-De, who are these children? And what is going on? Do you understand any of this?'

Lady Anastasia's eyes filled with fury. 'Harshender. Grab them.'

The soldier raced forward, surprisingly light and fast-moving for someone so heavy and powerful, but the two children ran in different directions, causing him to pause between them. Then he lunged swiftly to one side and grabbed Marko.

Marko wriggled in the man's thick arms and shouted out, 'We have a message for you from a friend. The information you are looking for is this: The girl's name is Annee, and you are looking for The Record of Ancient Mirrors.'

Hanshan did not respond.

'Shut the boy up,' Lady Anastasia shouted.

Harshender clamped his large hand over Marko's mouth.

Hanshan's eyes widened. He stared at the wriggling boy. 'You know something. You really know something that can help me.'

Mira echoed her brother's words. 'He's right. Listen to him. The person you are looking for is Annee and the object you seek is a book, the Record of Ancient Mirrors.'

Lady Anastasia was furious. 'They are lying. I am your wife. I am telling the truth. You have never even seen these children before.'

Hanshan turned to face her. 'I do not remember ever having seen you before either, good lady. But there is something in their words which strikes a distant chord in my heart. I need to know the truth.'

The woman said, 'Listen to me. The name you seek is mine. The name of your wife, your own true love. That's me, Anastasia.'

'And the object I seek?'

She looked nonplussed for a moment. And then she reached into the pouch at her waist. 'You seek this. It is a truth ring. It was our wedding ring.'

The stone started to glow red as she dropped it onto the stone table.

'You are lying,' Hanshan said quietly. 'I don't know how I know, but I do.'

'No. A red glow means I speak the truth,' Anastasia said. 'See how it glows red to confirm my words? If I was lying, it would glow blue.'

'It's the other way round,' revealed Mira. 'She's fooling you.'

Lady Anastasia grabbed the ring, took two broad strides and reached the girl. She grabbed her hand and pressed the crystal into it. The stone turned blue.

'See how this wicked child lies?' she asked. 'Now you must come with me. I will take you home.'

Hanshan remained still, unmoving and confused.

Anastasia grabbed his hand and started to pull him away. 'Harshender!' she commanded, 'get rid of those children and that man.'

'My pleasure, my lady,' said the soldier.

He grabbed Mira with his free hand and then dropped both children into a recessed corner of the cavern from where there was no chance of escape. Then he pulled out his broadsword.

'Time to go to sleep, children,' he growled. 'Forever!'

He lifted the sword and approached them.

'Do something!' Mira shouted. 'Use the mirror.'

'We haven't delivered our message successfully, though.'

'We tried! We're going to die. We gotta go.'

Marko reached behind him and pulled the Magic Mirror out of his school backpack. Mira took it from his hand and held it high, like a shield over their heads. The moonlight shone on it—and a glow appeared beneath it.

The two children closed their eyes.

But nothing happened. After a few seconds, Mira opened them. 'Uh-oh. The moon's gone!'

Marko looked at where she was gazing. Clouds had drifted over the moon, obscuring its light.

'Oops,' said the boy. 'We are dead meat.'

Harshender stepped towards them, the sword raised high.

'Wait!' The shouted word came from Hanshan. He broke free from Lady Anastasia. 'Don't hurt those children.'

He stepped towards them, his eyes moving rapidly as he tried to make sense of the scene. 'I remember this scene. The magic mirror, the light, the soldier, the anger. And I remember you being there, Lady Anastasia. And something very, very important.'

'Our wedding,' she said.

'No,' he said, shaking his head. 'Another woman. Annee.'

'Yes,' said Mira. 'Annee. And the Record of Ancient Mirrors.'

'The Record of Ancient Mirrors.'

He turned to glare at Lady Anastasia, apparently realising just how dangerous she was.

Mira decided to offer some advice. 'I would stay well away from that lady if I were you. She is not very ...'

But at that moment, there was an interruption: male voices could be heard from the main entrance. All eyes in the chamber turned to see who was approaching.

Brother Teh and the Healthy Skeptic stepped out of the cave opening into the mountaintop space, followed by the young monks from the class they taught. Behind them came several old men, including the old monk and the Ancient of Days. They were carrying lit torches, with waving red-white flames which created shifting, black-edged shadows behind them.

'There she is,' one of the young men shouted, pointing at Mira. 'Get her.'

'Oh brother,' said Mira. 'Am I having a bad day!'

Shi-De the cook stepped in front of the girl. 'What do you want with this child?'

Brother Teh said, 'She is a girl. She entered the training building and the chamber of ancients. She has defiled our premises. She dressed as a boy.'

'I didn't!' said Mira. 'Wait. Maybe I did. But I had to. We had a message to deliver.'

The healthy skeptic said, 'You admit your crime. You must be punished.'

The crowd of monks stepped towards the children, pushing the cook out of the way.

'Oh no,' said Mira. She and her brother held up the Magic Mirror again, keeping it as a shield against the approaching men.

But the clouds parted and moonlight flooded the chamber. The Magic Mirror amplified the light beneath Mira and Marko and they become lost in a super-bright glow.

'We're going home,' Marko said.

'Magic Mirror, HURRY UP,' said Mira.

As the brightness of the light narrowed their eyes, and then shut them, they heard a male voice calling out, 'Shi-De, farewell, do not forget me.'

And then the nameless poet called Cold Mountain leapt into the circle of light and stood between the two youngsters, holding the children by their shoulder, one on each side.

And then all three of them were gone.

11

Poetic Endings

The light became too bright and everything around them disappeared. They felt as if they were floating. The glare was so strong that they could feel it stinging their eyes even through their shut eyelids.

And then they could feel the floor beneath their feet, and the brightness began to fade.

Gradually the contours of a room appeared and came into focus. They were looking at the book-lined walls of grandfather's study.

'You came with us,' said Mira, her eyebrows raised.

'We've never had someone come with us before,' said Marko, looking at Hanshan. 'I didn't know people could.'

'Once before I travelled through the light of a magic mirror,' said the man in the tree-bark garments. 'I cannot recall the details, but I know they will come back to me.'

As soon as she felt fully returned to normal life, Mira stepped out of the range of the mirror Marko was holding high and slumped into Grandpa's armchair.

'*That* whole adventure,' she said, 'was a little too exciting for me.'

Her brother was slowly shaking his head in amazement. 'That was pretty cool,' he said. The boy turned to the man next to him. 'I think that horrible woman was trying to trick you but you realised what was happening at the end, right, Mr Hanshan?'

The man said, 'She was not my wife. Annee is my wife. I can feel the truth of that in my very bones. And the object I am seeking is the Record of Lost Mirrors, just as you said. Who asked you to pass on this information to me? It is important that I know.'

'Our grandfather,' said Marko. 'He told us you would need this information tonight and sent us to tell you.'

'Then you are all angels sent to help me.'

Mira shook her head. 'Not sure about that. Grandpa never tells us anything. He just sends us these jobs to do. He never gives us enough information.'

Her brother was looking a bit thoughtful. 'Yeah, but we do learn a lot,' he said. 'Like it was interesting to learn about poets, and ancient games and stuff, and the way we learnt it, we'll definitely never forget about it.'

Hanshan spoke with urgency in his voice. 'It is very

important that I find your grandfather. He may have important information for me.'

'Sorry,' said Marko. 'We don't know where he is. He left months ago, and didn't say where he was going. He sent us a package with these two books in it, but no clues as to where he was.'

Mira was also looking thoughtful.

'I just realised,' she said, 'I now have a cool prince-type dude living in my house. Do you mind if I show you off to all my friends at school? You don't have to talk to them or anything. Just like wave or something. Tell them you are a distant cousin of mine.'

But the man hardly appeared to be listening. He was gazing around the room. 'It's curious,' he breathed, talking to himself. 'I am sure I have never been here before, yet it feels like home in some strange way.'

'So you are going to stay, right?' asked Mira, excited.

'No,' said Hanshan. 'I have an urgent mission—to find Annee and the Record of Ancient Mirrors. I must go.'

Marko shook his head. 'You can't go. You don't know where to go.'

The man was pensive. 'I think it is not a matter of knowing where to go, but when to go. When I was on the Tiantai Mountain, I was in the right place, but at a different period of time. But where am I now? This house, is it on a mountain?'

The boy pondered. 'I don't think so. Or maybe it is. It is kind of sloped round here. But when a place is full of houses, it's hard to work out the original shape of the place, if you know what I mean.'

Mira was still anxious to try to hold on to this dynamic young man. 'But where are you going to go? You can't just call a taxi and tell the driver to take you to Annee. You probably need to travel through time or something.'

Something occurred to Marko and he suddenly looked worried. He grabbed the Magic Mirror of the Moon and placed it in his old school backpack. 'You can't use our Magic Mirror, sorry. We need it. Grandpa gave it to us and it's really important to us.'

Hanshan smiled. 'Fear not, young friends. I have no need of using your Magic Mirror. I have one of my own.'

From a large pouch that was built into the side of his stiff, tree-bark jacket, he pulled out a circular metal object.

'This is my Liu Bo board. I was holding it in my hands when I first arrived on the mountain.'

'Your game board,' said Mira. 'I know all about the history of games. That was one of the earliest games.'

Hanshan gazed at the disk of polished metal. 'I have always known that this was important. When I found myself on the mountain at first, I had nothing at all—no memory of who I was or even what my name was. But I had this object with me, so I knew it was important—it was the key to who I was and where I came from. I remember using it as a weapon. I felt that it had saved my life somehow. So I have always treasured it. I knew it was a mirror, and I knew that it was a game board. But I never realised that it could be a portal too, until now.'

'All mirrors are portals,' Marko said suddenly.

His sister turned to stare at him. 'That's a bit deep, coming from you,' she said. 'Where did you get that thought from?'

'I read it in a poem,' the boy said.

***

When the children woke up the next day, Hanshan had gone. The previous night, they had gone to bed, leaving him going through the books and papers and objects in Grandpa's study, trying to find clues as to who he was, and where he belonged.

'He was probably up all night,' said Mira, rubbing sleep-dust out of her eyes.

'I hope he found some useful information,' her brother added.

The house was empty—so, presumably, Hanshan had vanished. But it was impossible to tell whether he had simply walked out of the front door or used his own magic mirror to transport himself to a different time and place.

Full of memories of their adventure, they ate some breakfast noodles quietly, each absently staring at the books they had been given.

Then Marko turned a page and laughed.

'What's funny?' asked his sister.

But her brother kept laughing. 'That is so weird,' he said.

'What?'

'Well, do you know that those monks were wondering which two among them would become immortals and live forever?'

'Yeah.'

'Do you know which pair it was?'

'I think I can guess. Hanshan and Shi-De are the ones, right?'

Marko nodded. 'Yep. The two people they would least expect to become immortals, I'm sure.'

'Life's like that.'

Marko showed her the pictures of a pair of laughing poets and some writing in Chinese characters in the book.

Mira read the text next to the pictures. 'The two vagabond poets of Cold Mountain became classified as immortals, and went on to inspire people around the world. They were known as the Tang Dynasty poets, producing their main works around AD 670. In China, they are known as Hanshan and Shi-De. In Japan, they are known as Kanzan and Jittoku. In the rest of the world, they are known through a collection of Hanshan's works under the title Cold Mountain. In the western world, they were particularly celebrated for inspiring the writings of Jack Kerouac and Gary Snyder, a pair of writers who were members of what is known as The Beat Generation in the late 1950s and early 1960s.'

After breakfast, they went to Grandpa's study. Hanshan had taken his mirror, as theirs—the Magic Mirror of the Moon—was still in Marko's red backpack.

Mira took it out to see if anything had changed. She knew that words sometimes magically appeared on the outer rim of the mirror.

The last time she looked, there were five words. But now a sixth had appeared: 'Look time coming devil woman creature.'

'It's warning us about a dangerous woman,' said Mira.

'Lady Anastasia?' asked Marko.

His sister nodded. 'Probably. I have a feeling we haven't heard the last of her.'

Marko put down his book and Mira picked it up. 'Can I read this now? I've always loved poetry.'

AUTHORS' NOTE

Except for the members of the Lee family and their associates, all the historical material in this book is true.

There really is a Guoqing Temple on Mount Tiantai, which is in Zhejiang Province, China.

And many years ago, around AD 600, there really were a couple of troublemakers living there. One was a nameless poet known only by his address: Cold Mountain, which is Hanshan in Chinese. The other was a man named Shi-De who was the cook at the monastery. They were both known for their laughter and fondness for tricking people—including their greatest fan, a government official.

The pair really did write poems and became known as Immortals. Cold Mountain is certainly believed to have written poems on rocks, trees and walls, rather than paper.

And he really did inspire Jack Kerouac and Gary Snyder, the 'Beat Generation' writers of the Western world. Kerouac really did write a book on a single sheet of paper, as long as nine cars!

Liubo and Go are among the most ancient of games which inspired Chess and other games which are widely played today.

And most important of all, magic mirrors really exist. By that, we mean that there really are ancient metal mirrors with strange properties which have baffled scientists for hundreds of years.

Why not try to find one, the next time you are in a museum?

All the Magic Mirror stories are based on real events in history. As a result, we have great fun researching them and writing them, and we learn so much, too. We hope you feel the same!

Luther Tsai and Nury Vittachi

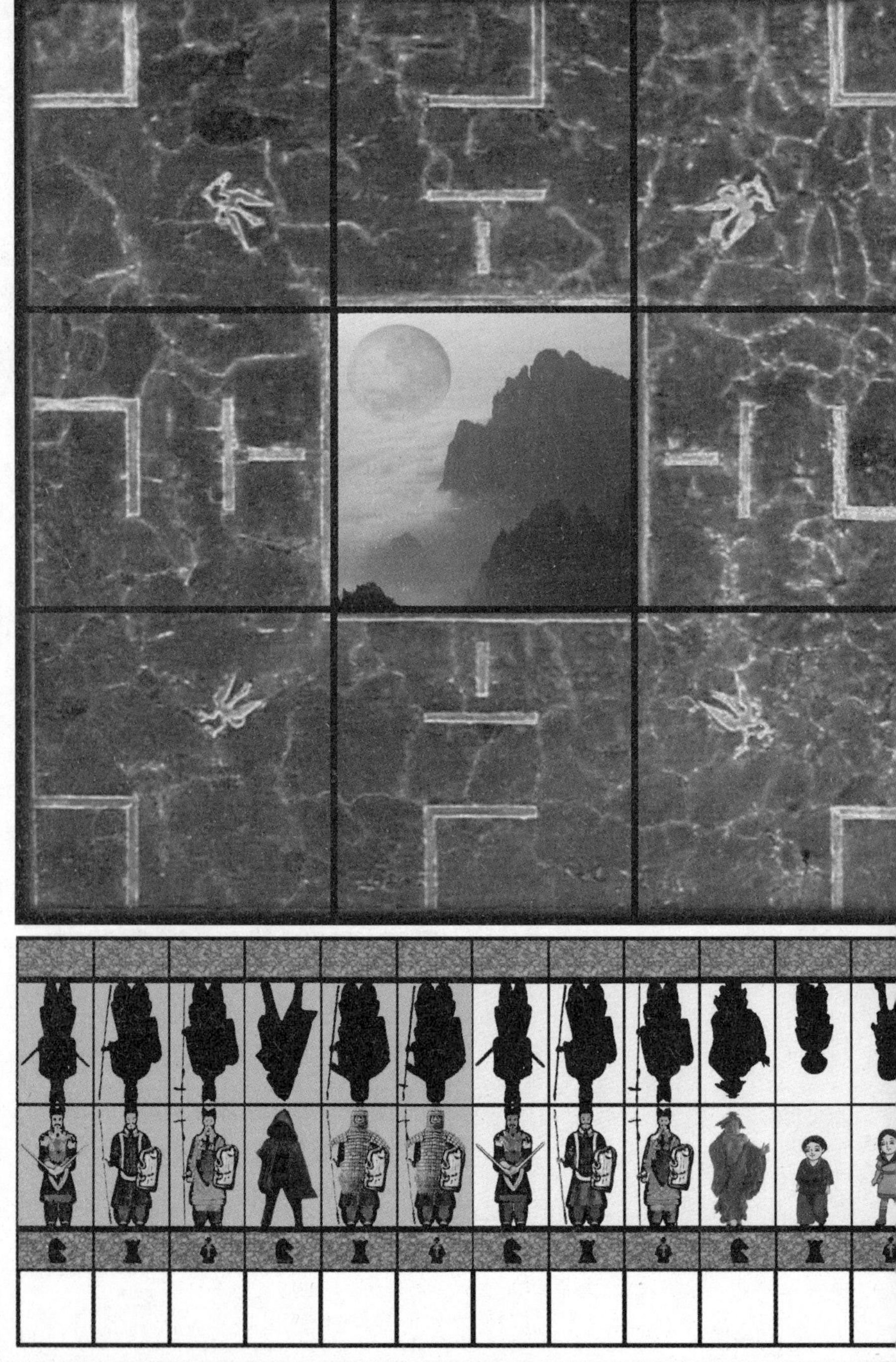

Liubo is an ancient Chinese game that appeared in history 4000 years ago but whose real origin is found *in myths about mysterious 'TLV' gameboard patterns engraved on the back of bronze mirrors once used to peer into the future.* The rules of the game are lost in time but Liubo is said to be an ancestor of Chinese and Western Chess, reflecting a cosmic game played by Immortals.

UBO BOARD: Reflections of Eternity

: distinctive 'TLV' Liubo gameboard pattern first appeared on back of ancient mirrors. *No one knows which came first, the stical Game of Immortals or the Magic Mirror?*

E COSMIC CHASE

e a Shadow, she wrapped herself in darkness to find her 'ennium old prey - Han Shan - always the lovestruck poet. e Shadow will send him back into black eternity with her Ghost diers. Can Marko and Mira find Han Shan and save him?

D MOUNTAIN LIUBO

The sides of SHADOW and LIGHT begin as shown in a twilight zone of three by three squares. Their unique powers and moves are the same as Western Chess pieces (**Bishop** diagonal any number of spaces/**Rook** orthogonal any number of spaces/**Knight** 'L' shape move as shown:

The Shadow seeks to checkmate Han Shan, and Mira and Marko must work together to checkmate The Shadow before that happens! Rules for check and checkmating the king in Chess apply to the Shadow and Han Shan who move as Knights. ***Whoever checkmates the Knight piece wins!!***

en captured, the owner of the piece may 'teleport' it to ***any empty*** *square on* ***any*** *following turn, tead of moving a piece on the board. WATCH OUT! Captured enemies can come back to haunt you!*

gal Moves: 1) **Cannot repeat moves** back and forth between same squares 2) On the **First Move** ther side may move The Shadow or Han Shan *(Moving from initial setup, they would be captured and ckmated by either the Bishop or Rook in the next move!)*

tional Battlegame: ***Before capturing*** a piece players may try their hand at influencing destiny by tling "Rock-Scissors-Stone". If the attacker loses he ***retreats*** to the space she came from.

ADOW PIECES
ded Lady (Knight)
ost Army Soldier (Bishop)
ost Army Soldier (Rook)

LIGHT PIECES
Han Shan (Knight)
Mira (Bishop)
Marko (Rook)

Chess Piece Assembly
Cut-out pieces and fold M (mountain convex fold) and V (valley concave fold) and glue with bases. Setup board to save Han Shan but beware The Shadow!

OTHER BOOKS IN THIS SERIES

Magic Mirror

Mysteries...

The Traveller's Tale

LUTHER TSAI & NURY VITTACHI

SCHOLASTIC

Magic Mirror

Mysteries...

The Tomb of Time

LUTHER TSAI & NURY VITTACHI

SCHOLASTIC

Magic Mirror

Mysteries...

The Wall of Willows

LUTHER TSAI & NURY VITTACHI

SCHOLASTIC

Magic Mirror
Mysteries...
The Shining Scripture
LUTHER TSAI & NURY VITTACHI
SCHOLASTIC

V
M
V
M